Science

Concepts in Social Thought

Series Editor: Frank Parkin

Published Titles

Concepts in Social Thought

Science

Steve Fuller

University of Minnesota Press
Minneapolis

Copyright © Steve Fuller 1997

First published by Open University Press 1997

Published simultaneously in the United States 1997
by the University of Minnesota Press
111 Third Avenue South, Suite 290,
Minneapolis, MN 55401-2520

http://www.upress.umn.edu

Printed in Great Britain

Library of Congress Cataloging-in-Publication Data

A catalog record for this book is available from the Library of Congress

ISBN 0-8166-3124-7 (hc)
ISBN 0-8166-3125-5 (pb)

The University of Minnesota is an
equal-opportunity educator and employer.

Contents

Preface

It is testimony to Justin Vaughan's publishing skills that, after a brief conversation in Durham in December 1995, he convinced me to add this book to my overburdened writing schedule. If the reader comes away thinking that the idea and institution of 'science' go to the very heart of what the social sciences are about, then it will have served its purpose. In composing the book I have substantially reworked material that first appeared as part of articles in the following journals: *Futures, History of Human Sciences, Interdisciplinary Science Reviews, Journal of Mind and Behavior, Science in Context, Social Studies of Science, Social Text,* and *Theory, Culture and Society.* I thank the editors for allowing me to develop my frequently outrageous ideas in their esteemed forums. In recent years my thinking about these matters has been animated by the research and debates surrounding multicultural knowledge. I have been aided by the writings and speakings of Ahmed Bouzid, Mammo Muchie, Zia Sardar and – most recently – Dhruv Raina. Related to this strand is my long-standing interest in world-systems theory, prompted by a free journal exchange between Immanuel Wallerstein's *Review* and my own *Social Epistemology.* In the summer of 1996, Mitch Allen helped to crystallize my thoughts on this corpus by giving me the opportunity to preview what promises to be Andre Gunder Frank's *magnum opus*, which in turn led to a fruitful electronic correspondence with Frank about the role of science and technology in Europe's recent global ascent. On matters more straightforwardly related to the history of science, I have benefited from the wisdom of Lewis Pyenson and Skuli Sigurdsson. Since moving to the United Kingdom in 1994, I have become involved in issues relating to the 'public understanding of science' and science education more generally. My former students Jim Collier, Kirk Junker and Joan Leach have moved me increasingly in this direction. Before I forget, I must thank my fellow 'Science Warriors', Andrew Ross, Paul Gross, Norman Levitt, Bill Keith, John Angus Campbell, Harry Collins, Adrian Melott, Phil Baringer, Steven Weinberg, Lewis Wolpert and even that consummate hoaxer Alan Sokal – all of whom, despite their very considerable differences of opinion, take the future of science sufficiently seriously to be taken seriously themselves. Needless to say, in this book I hardly expect to have satisfied all the wishes and expectations of such a diverse group of influences. But luckily I know someone who is very tolerant of contradictions: Sujatha Raman, my favourite dialectician and virtual coauthor, to whom this book is dedicated.

Steve Fuller
Durham, 1997

The Public Understanding of Science: Our Latest Moral Panic

For the past few years, the ides of March in Britain have marked the beginning of a spring ritual known as 'Science Week'. First, a flurry of surveys are conducted to find out what the 'average person' – an unsuspecting weekend shopper in a London suburb – thinks about science. The results, usually a source of horror for readers of the national broadsheet newspapers, are then used to kick off a steady stream of public lectures, experimental demonstrations, and museum exhibits, all designed to promote the cause of 'Science' in the barnstorming style that was popular in the nineteenth century. The official government reason for holding Science Week is that student enrolments in natural science courses (including teacher training courses) have been dropping steadily over the past decade, a trend that is thought to be somehow related to the perceived decline of British technological innovation and industrial productivity.

Much of the hoopla surrounding Science Week has the feel of *moral panic*; a breakdown in social order, the nature of which is neither understood nor controlled by those in charge. The temptation, then, is to scapegoat a relatively defenceless group who somehow can be made to symbolize the crisis. Thus, primary and secondary school science teachers with degrees in education rather than in one of the natural sciences are often made scapegoats for not sparking the spirit of enquiry in the classroom. Occasionally someone will observe that the decline in enrolments may not be such a bad idea, given that students in the natural sciences are now just as unlikely to find work related to their field as students in the humanities and social sciences. Nevertheless, defenders of Science Week maintain that the malaise runs deeper. Surveys show that people have only the vaguest idea of what 'science' or 'the scientific method' is supposed to be. For example, only one in seven respondents mention 'theory construction' or 'hypothesis testing' as part of the scientific method.[1] Moreover, the public cannot fathom what makes such seemingly disparate disciplines as palaeontology, high-energy physics, industrial chemistry, and genetic engineering equally 'scientific', and hence worthy of their sustained interest and support. When it comes to specific research projects, the public seems benign towards inexpensive research that is unlikely to interfere with their daily lives but insists on the accountability of any research that is likely to result in a substantial change of lifestyle. In the latter case, the public seems to have a much more vivid sense of what might constitute such research than scientists themselves normally do.

Does the public understanding of science, as characterized above, constitute a genuine state of crisis, or has the scientific community itself misunderstood something significant about the social conditions that enable its continued existence? An important lesson of this book is that the latter is the case, and that the public's instinctive response to science is fundamentally sound and hence merits further exploration. There is no 'scientific method', unless one means the attempt to use one successful form of inquiry as the model for them all. Even then, 'success' is a concept fraught with difficulties, involving a rather complicated relationship between science and its history. As to why all the disciplines of the natural sciences have come to be regarded as 'sciences', the answer is to be found more in how these fields came to be institutionalized than in anything that these fields' practices might have in common. Indeed, the identity of science has become so unstable in the contemporary world that it makes sense to ask whether knowledge production (as opposed to sublimated politics or subsidized employment) is the primary social function of such highly publicized pieces of scientific research as the Human Genome Project, the (ill-fated) Superconducting Supercollider and the Hubble Space Telescope. Moreover, not only *can* this question be asked, it already *has* been – especially by policymakers who ask, of science, *cui bono*? Who should be doing what, in what setting, to what end(s), for whose benefit and at what cost to whom? This series of questions constitutes the *normative* dimension of scientific enterprise. The systematic attempt to address them is called *social epistemology*.[2] In response to these questions, the following arguments have become increasingly conspicuous in recent years:

1 If scientific knowledge is indeed a 'public good', then the government needs to scrutinize both the rate and the distribution of return on the public's investment in science.
2 If scientific knowledge is not a public good, then special interest groups should invest in the sorts of inquiries that are most likely to serve their respective constituencies. This will involve considerations of both the process by which knowledge is produced and the products themselves. In addition, raising the support needed to produce a favoured form of knowledge may require expanding the base of the constituency through proselytizing and marketing.
3 There is no reason why the devolution of labour in our 'postindustrial society' from tenured, salaried employment to more temporary piecework should not equally apply to intellectual pursuits. In fact, historically speaking, it is by no means clear that those who pursue continuous academic careers turn out to be the most significant knowledge producers.
4 The increase in disciplinary specialization over the course of the twentieth century has had more to do with the ability of universities and other academic institutions to insulate themselves from political and economic pressures than to an internal trajectory of 'growth through functional differentiation' of the knowledge base. If anything, academic guild barriers prove to hinder rather than help in addressing persistent social and economic problems that require the coordination of different expertise.

These arguments share an interesting characteristic. If we use *epistemic* to mean that the pursuit of inquiry or production of knowledge is a distinct and privileged enterprise, the arguments are *post-epistemic*.[3] They refuse to confer any special privilege on knowledge production or inquiry as a social practice: whatever normative strictures apply to social practices in general, they apply specifically to scientific practices as well. Thus, instead of a norm traditionally associated with the pursuit of knowledge, such as 'maximize the number of true beliefs while minimizing the number of false ones', the four arguments contain implicit appeals to normative standards that are more familiar from other spheres of social life. Thus, we find imperatives to maximize, respectively: 1 benefit-to-cost ratio; 2 relevance; 3 productivity; and 4 adaptability.

Since the reader may already begin to feel the ground slipping beneath them, let me explain the philosophical and sociological orientations that inform this book. Philosophically, I propose that we think of science in the same spirit as we normally think of *democracy*. Sociologically, I propose that we think about science from the standpoint of an *outsider*. Let me briefly justify each proposal before proceeding any further.

There is general agreement among students of politics that democracy is a vexed concept whose history is more a series of fits and starts than a continuous upward trajectory. While it is easy to imagine democracy thriving in relatively small homogeneous communities where political accountability is a matter of personal honour, it is much harder to envisage this idea translated into large, complex, heterogeneous societies. Thus, political theorists routinely query whether it makes sense to speak of 'democracy' once public participation is limited to the selection of representatives who, among themselves, legislate for the entire polity.[4] That concerns about the feasibility of democracy should inform an account of science is not as far-fetched as it first sounds, since most democratic theorists in the Western tradition – the American founding fathers, John Stuart Mill, John Dewey, Karl Popper and Jürgen Habermas immediately come to mind – have regarded the form of critical inquiry that characterizes science as the model of the ideal polity. The only problem – and it is a big one – is whether the model is limited to an elite whose internal divisions mirror the interests in society at large or whether the model can be extended to include everyone's direct participation.

The problem becomes more pressing as society becomes larger and more complex. However, we can identify two general solution strategies, *Little Democracy* and *Big Democracy*, which approximate the views of Jean-Jacques Rousseau (1712–78) and John Stuart Mill (1806–73), respectively. A good way of thinking about the difference between these two strategies is in terms of two questions. What is the image of social order appropriate to democracy,

	Political style	*Ends*	*Means*
Little Democracy	Participatory	Consensus	Devolution
Big Democracy	Representative	Open-mindedness	Interaction

Figure 1.1 Little Democracy and Big Democracy.

and how is this image best realized in an expanding society? Answers to these two questions – about, respectively, the ends and means of democracy – are displayed in Figure 1.1.

The main virtue of Little Democracy is that its members hold a sufficient number of beliefs and values in common to agree on courses of action, the consequences of which they are willing to collectively bear and learn from. Accordingly, when the size of the polity exceeds its ability to secure such a consensus, the Little Democrat believes that it should be devolved into smaller units within which the relevant background commitments can be secured. In contrast, order in Big Democracy is a dialectic of countervailing interests, which do not pretend to be aiming at a course of action that will suit everyone optimally. However, focused interaction promises to temper natural differences of perspective, as the various interested parties learn to scrutinize each other's claims and advance claims of their own that can sustain scrutiny. Whereas the Little Democrat worries that lack of consensus would undermine the solidarity needed for effective collective action, the Big Democrat worries that lack of open-mindedness would lead to the sort of authoritarian 'groupthink' that has historically led oppressed minorities to revolt. Thus, instinctively, Little Democrats are *communists* and Big Democrats *liberals*.

In contemporary philosophy of science, the rationales behind Little Democracy and Big Democracy resemble the famous debate between Thomas Kuhn (1922–96) and Karl Popper (1902–94) at the London School of Economics in 1965 over whether science was more a 'closed' or an 'open' society.[5] However, as this book endeavours to show, strict analogies between Little Democracy and Kuhnian paradigms, on the one hand, and between Big Democracy and Popperian critical rationalism, on the other, are misleading, once we consider not only the constitution of science as a polity, but science's relationship to the larger polity. Here we find a further polarization of the two models of democracy, as communism shades into *totalitarianism*, while liberalism veers towards *libertarianism*.

Because what we are talking about is called 'science' rather than, say, 'ideology', these political terms may sound a bit strong. Nevertheless, the social processes that they presuppose are largely the same. Thus, Kuhn's Little Democracy image of science has been historically aligned with a view that once scientists agree on a paradigm to serve as the basis for further inquiry, the paradigm should be presented to the larger society as self-contained expertise to which the public should defer on relevant occasions (if they are incapable of directly acquiring the expertise). In this way, scientists kill two birds with one stone: they retain their autonomy by displaying their authority. We shall identify this move as the calling card of the *Positivist* interpretation of science.[6] In contrast, Popper's Big Democracy image of science is more closely associated with the view that what scientists take to be 'knowledge' is only a waystation in the path of inquiry, and hence one should expect that epistemic agreements reached by scientific elites will be modified and perhaps even resisted to suit the needs and experiences of specific communities. However strong the potential for knowledge to become fragmented under such circumstances, it must nevertheless be granted that when non-elite knowers alter the knowledge handed down by the scientific elites, they are simply applying to their own cases the spirit of critical inquiry that had enabled the elites to break away from traditional modes of thought in the first place. This is the mark of the *Enlightenment* interpretation of science. It breaks down the hierarchical relationships between 'basic' and 'applied' science, not to mention the relative contributions that 'research' and 'teaching' make to knowledge production in society.

Of course, the historical Enlightenment fell far short of this truly democratic ideal. After all, Voltaire (1694–1778) and Denis Diderot (1713–84) never found it necessary to distinguish between whether they wanted people to simply *respect* or actually *become* scientists, since mere respect for science sufficed to ensure that the emerging middle class of eighteenth century France bought subscriptions to their great collective project, *L'Encyclopédie*. Nevertheless, the Enlightenment at its best – as when Diderot explored the dynamic features of nature that escaped the grasp of Newtonian mechanics – exemplified what Immanuel Kant (1724–1804) saw as the movement's 'dare to know' spirit.[7] This spirit is eminently worth preserving and cultivating, but is today on the verge of extinction. The reason for this unfortunate turn of events (or at least the one presupposed in these pages) is a version of the thesis that Joseph Schumpeter (1883-1950) proposed for the slow but inevitable death of capitalism.[8] According to Schumpeter, the lifeblood of capitalism is entrepreneurship, that is, people who seek to 'creatively destroy' the market with technological innovations that displace existing relations between producers and consumers. These shocks to the economic system are registered as business cycles, which as capitalism expands become increasingly costly not only to the firms that are disadvantaged by a successful innovator but also to the state, which must provide for the welfare of the people whose livelihoods are displaced by a new fluctuation in the market. Consequently, both government and business have an interest in containing innovation within certain bounds in order to stabilize the market. This inevitably leads to a planned economy that removes the element of risk that nurtures the entrepreneurial spirit. Schumpeter's core insight was thus to reverse the gestalt of innovation, so as to emphasize its *costs* (how much and to whom?) rather than its benefits, and to argue that it is the costs, and not the benefits, that in the end determine society's tolerance for innovation. In this book, the reader is encouraged to explore the implications of the Schumpeterian scenario, when the relevant innovations are in science rather than technology; it is the constructively critical inquirer, instead of the creatively destructive entrepreneur, who is threatened with extinction in the ever expanding world of 'Big Science'.

To explain the sociological orientation of this book – that of the outsider looking in on science – let me first review the spirit in which the past two decades of work in the sociology of science has been conducted. During this time, the calling card of field practitioners has been an empiricist rhetoric that claims to open the doors of those scientific sanctuaries, the laboratories, and invites intelligent readers to judge for themselves what they observe.[9] This rhetoric invokes democratic and scientific themes simultaneously; everyone can be their own 'scientist of science' by exercising a level of perceptual acuity that is evenly distributed across the population. And what is it that one sees in those hallowed halls of science? As it turns out, one does *not* see the sordid dealings associated with the recent cases of fraud in the world of biological science. On the contrary, 'science in action' is much more *ordinary* than its levels of material and spiritual support in our society would suggest. The public's understanding of science, as described at the start of this chapter, instinctively captures this sentiment, and recent sociology of science has tried to articulate it by showing that science can be understood using the concepts that social scientists normally use to understand the rest of society. Sociologists are thus routinely faced with the methodological irony that because we normally think about science as different from the rest of society, in order to think about science as a normal social activity we need to become estranged from our normal attitude towards it.

But perhaps even more ironic is that the sociologist's ability to get behind the scenes of the laboratory is primarily a literary one, and specifically a competence in the rhetoric of 'virtual witnessing', in Steven Shapin's phrase. It relies on readers to trust the sociologist's veracity to roughly the same degree as they would normally trust scientists' accounts of their work. The result has been to disrupt the usual image of science as a monolith of rationality. Even readers who doubt sociology's ability to provide a definitive answer to the nature of science typically come away from a sociological study more open-minded about what science might be. From the perspective of social epistemology, that is half the battle won, since the ability to entertain alternative visions of science is a prerequisite to any serious public discussion of the social disposition of science. All too often, it seems, the public is given only one set of lenses with which to observe contemporary science: the rose-coloured spectacles of science's long and progressive past. The obvious dissimilarities between, say, an Ancient Greek poem on the nature of things and a $10,000,000,000 particle accelerator is papered over by the appearance of a 'common quest' in which the former somehow culminates in the latter. Even Kuhn's very influential *Structure of Scientific Revolutions* (1970), a work avowedly attuned to the social character of science, continues to leave something of the same impression, as the relatively autonomous cycle of paradigms and revolutions obscures any sense of how science changes in response to developments in politics, industry, religion, or any other institution. An important aim of this book, then, is to show how an enriched understanding of the history of science – one that takes in the perspectives other cultures and even (in Chapter

4) another planet – can help us to construct a public understanding of science with which we can live, or at least get to grips.

There are two rather different ways of conceptualizing the sort of open-mindedness towards science that sociological inquiry can provide.[10] Let us call the first the *inside out* perspective, since its rhetoric is that of the sociologist spreading the good news of what she has found in the laboratory. Probably the one favoured by most sociologists of science, its philosophical inspiration is drawn from Ludwig Wittgenstein (1889–1951). The idea is that if people accepted science for what it is rather than for what it cannot be – namely, the elixir of all social ills – then both scientists and the public would behave much more sanely towards each other. Once we get past the laboratory doors, we find that a scientist is simply someone trained to do certain useful things in certain places and committed to seeing the world in certain useful ways, just like any other professional. It is in this sense that scientists deserve to be accorded respect. Scientists themselves have been the quickest to pick up on the main problem with this image of *scientist as citizen*.[11] It implies that science has been oversold, which opens the door to funding cuts and other disruptions to scientists' livelihoods.

The second view, one more closely aligned with the Marxist tradition in the sociology of knowledge, focuses on the dialectical relationship between what scientists do and what they (and others) say they do. This perspective starts by agreeing with the scientists that simply revealing the ordinary nature of scientists' work does little more than add to the mystery of science's exalted social standing. However, it parts company with the scientists over what is missing. Let us call this perspective *outside in* because of the role it assigns to non-scientists[12] in authorizing scientific knowledge. Put somewhat crudely, the day non-scientists stop believing that science makes reference to a reality outside the laboratory, science will devolve into a marginal social practice that is part sport, part ritual. We often forget that we are always making judgements about the validity and relevance of scientific knowledge, even though very few of us have any deep understanding of what it is that we are passing judgement on.[13] Although this *citizen-as-scientist* perspective is not an especially pretty epistemological vantage point, it is nevertheless the one that is more consonant with the ideal of democratic accountability for science.[14]

My own sympathies lie with the second perspective, mainly

because I believe that most of what non-scientists need to know in order to make informed public judgements about science fall under the rubric of history, philosophy, and sociology of science, rather than the technical content of scientific subjects. In that spirit, Chapter 2 reflects on the characteristics that tend to distinguish the natural sciences from the social sciences. These include different attitudes towards criticism, history, and language. Chapter 3 considers the conceptual histories of 'science', 'scientific', and 'scientist' by looking at the social relations in which the use of these words have been embedded. In Chapter 4, we confront the ultimate outsider perspective, with a team of Martian anthropologists who hit upon the idea of applying categories from the sociology of religion to understand the attitudes and practices surrounding that 'quasi-fictional entity', science. Their recently discovered report also contains appendices that put perverse spins on the most famous sociological account of scientific norms and the *Science Citation Index*. Chapter 5 provides a theoretical discussion of alternative historical perspectives on science, contrasting histories that stress its inevitable onward march and those that make key developments appear more like accidents whose consequences may have been overrated. We begin to see clearly the interrelationship between the history of science and that of religion, politics, and the economy. In Chapter 6, we consider, specifically, the ways in which Islam and Japan provide alternative outsider perspectives on the sense and import of science's 'autonomy' from the rest of Western society. Islam has consistently stressed the recklessness of Western science as born of a lack of value-direction, and Japan's early encounters with modern science offer, in both word and deed, a critique of the superstitious nature of the West's beliefs about its own history. Finally, Chapter 7 considers the dismal prospect that science's increasing involvement with the material basis of society is sapping its spirit of critical inquiry and perhaps even presaging the dawn of a new 'Oriental Despotism' administered by high-tech, subcontracted knowledge workers.

Notes

1 These results were originally published in *Nature* (Durant *et al.* 1989), following a survey of over 2000 Britons on their views of science. A

good cross-cultural cross-section of research in this area is Lewenstein (1992). Also see the quarterly journal, *Public Understanding of Science*.

2 See especially Fuller (1988, 1993a, b). My own brand of social epistemology locates the normative metatheory of scientific knowledge in politics and ethics, not epistemology as it is predominately practised in analytic philosophy. Alternative philosophical approaches to social epistemology are critiqued in Fuller (1996b).

3 I have discussed the 'post-epistemic attitude' in Fuller (1994a, b). It is also a theme running through Fuller (1993b). Much of my thinking along these lines is indebted to Ravetz's (1971) conception of 'post-normal' science, in which inquiry is driven by concerns extraneous to what Kuhn (1970) called 'the logic of puzzle-solving'. Ravetz's book is a classic of 1960s-inspired 'critical science', which mobilized the history, philosophy and sociology of science to challenge science's involvement in the 'military–industrial complex'.

4 Dahl (1989).

5 The debate appears in Lakatos & Musgrave (1970).

6 It has become a truism in the philosophy of science to speak of Kuhn as having deposed the Positivist image of inquiry. Unfortunately, neither Kuhn nor the Positivists saw matters this way, which is why Kuhn (1970) was published as the final instalment of the *International Encyclopedia of Unified Science*. See Fuller (1998) for a full excavation and systematic critique of Kuhn.

7 On the context and implications of Kant's injunction, see Schmidt (1996: 58–64).

8 Schumpeter (1945).

9 Latour and Woolgar (1986) exemplifies this genre.

10 The following contrast corresponds, respectively, to the deep/shallow science distinction developed in Fuller (1993b: 11–16).

11 A recent popularization in this vein that has stirred considerable public controversy is Collins and Pinch (1993).

12 'Non-scientist' means here anyone who is not competent in the *specific* science in question. In other words, if quantum mechanics is the topic of dicussion, an evolutionary biologist (along with every other non-specialist) counts as a 'non-scientist'. It would be interesting to conduct a 'public understanding of science' survey on the depth of scientific understanding that scientists have of areas outside their specialties – to see how much better it is than that of the 'lay' public.

13 If this point does not strike the reader as immediately obvious, consider the following activities: scanning cereal boxes for their nutritional content, second-guessing one's physician about whether to take the assigned dosage of medicine, inspecting the engine of an automobile, etc.

14 Taylor (1996) is a good textbook in this approach.

2

The Sociological Peculiarity of the Natural Sciences

When people talk about 'the scientific method', they usually mean a procedure whose natural home is classical mechanics, the branch of physics that came of age 300 years ago in the work of Isaac Newton (1642–1727). It purports to explain the movement of visible objects over a certain space in a given time, not only on Earth but throughout the entire known universe. Although Newton himself might contest the exact description, his method supposedly proceeded by hypothesizing a bold generalization that aspired to the status of 'natural law', on the basis of which one could predict that certain things would happen on certain occasions. One would then set up an 'experiment' to test the prediction. Originally, an experiment was conceived primarily in terms of treating nature as a laboratory, but later the roles were reversed, so that nowadays the laboratory is treated as a surrogate for nature. We can get a sense of the pervasiveness of this 'Newtonian' style of thinking by observing that as late as the first half of the twentieth century, primary and secondary school teachers in the USA were routinely taught about the scientific method from a small book by the great pragmatist philosopher, John Dewey (1859–1952), under the presumptuous title, *How We Think* (1908). Here a common-sense problem such as explaining the movement of soap bubbles in a newly washed glass tumbler was treated as a watered-down version of an exercise from a classical mechanics textbook.[1]

To be sure, scientists themselves – usually non-physicists – have decried this account of the scientific method as a caricature. One such scientist is Stephen Jay Gould, a Harvard palaeontologist who is in the top echelon of science popularizers writing in the English language today.[2] His spiritual ancestor is not Newton, but that other great scientific icon, Charles Darwin (1809–82), the founder of modern evolutionary theory. If the formidable mathematical apparatus of Newton's work delineated the Creator's steady hand, Darwin's stylish English prose lured the Victorian reader into accepting nature's order as the product of a series of glorified accidents that left the existence of the Creator completely open. Whereas in classical mechanics 'history' is something that can be predicted, knowing only the laws of physics and the state of the universe at a point prior to the predicted event, in evolutionary theory one cannot determine the range of possible futures without knowing everything that had happened prior to the event in question.

Gould's objection points to a salient fact about the fields that are encompassed by the 'natural sciences'. They actually have rather little in common, at least if we judge these matters by what people who call themselves 'scientists' do for a living. An experimental physicist works in the highly controlled setting of a laboratory that is designed to filter out the idiosyncrasies of the everyday world, and an evolutionary biologist examines organisms fossilized in rocks or living in their native habitats, in either case careful not to ignore the distinctive features of organic existence. Indeed, there seems to be nothing 'natural' about grouping physicists and biologists under the general rubric of 'natural science', at least when compared with the similarity and overlap of interests displayed among the fields we normally associate with the 'social sciences', such as psychology, economics, political science, and sociology This point was not lost on the first modern *epistemologists*: philosophical theorists of knowledge who wrote at the turn of the twentieth century in Germany, the nation whose university system was the first to officially recognize disciplinary specialization as an irreversible fact of academic life. Although these philosophers – Wilhelm Dilthey (1833–1911), Wilhelm Windelband (1848–1915), and Heinrich Rickert (1863–1936) – are now largely known only to other specialists, their combined wisdom comes in handy at this point. They tried to meet the challenge posed by John Stuart Mill in *A System of Logic* (1843), namely, that any difference in style between Newtonian mechanics and other fields of inquiry was simply a sign of the latter's epistemic immaturity. Once biology, say, or, for that matter, sociology became a full-fledged science, it would sport general laws just like physics.

An extreme claim of this sort invites extreme responses, and hence many humanists and social scientists have come to embrace Windelband's position that the search for general laws applies only to the natural sciences because the things they study do not vary over time and space. Unfortunately, Windelband does little to help the likes of Gould and other post-Darwinian naturalists, who believe that history is an essential feature of their disciplines. For his part, Dilthey drew on the largely negative definition of nature as 'raw material' or 'inert matter' that had been advanced by the idealist tradition in German philosophy. Accordingly, 'nature' was simply that which resists the striving of the human spirit: something whose workings can only be known 'from the outside' for purposes of human prediction and control. This metaphysical sensibility, in turn, explained the traditional connection between the natural sciences and purely instrumental, or technological, conceptions of knowledge. In any case, the natural sciences did not permit the sort of understanding that can be gained by getting under someone's skin. Dilthey grounded this special capacity of 'understanding' in the biological unity of the human species.

Finally, Rickert pushed Dilthey's train of thought still further, arguing that the only real difference between the sciences lay not in what they studied, but in the value-orientation of the scientist. In that sense, *anything* could be studied as a natural or, in Rickert's terms, 'cultural' science, depending on whether the categories used by the scientist were ones that could be used by the entities under study to promote their own ends. Thus, much the same evidence about the human condition can be organized into two radically different sorts of sciences. One would look like cultural anthropology in using categories that operate at the level at which people give meaning to their lives and the other more like sociobiology, which appeals to genetic and ecological factors that are typically outside people's ordinary sphere of consciousness. However, Rickert did not stop to consider that as a 'scientific' mentality seeped into everyday life, people might incorporate genetic and ecological considerations into their ordinary understanding. Indeed, Rickert's most famous doctoral student, the great existentialist philosopher Martin Heidegger (1889–1976), did his best to make such seepage appear alien to the human spirit.

Interestingly, this gradual philosophical recognition of the internal diversity of science has not thrown the natural sciences into the sort of interdisciplinary strife that is a matter of course in the social sciences. We can examine this matter from various angles, which together give us a glimpse into the sociological peculiarity of the natural sciences.

First, it is important to recognize that natural scientists have periodically made concerted efforts at resolving their disagreements over the aims and methods of their inquiries, at least to the satisfaction of most of the practitioners concerned. There is no clearer case in point than the unification of biology in the 1930s under the so-called neo-Darwinian synthesis, which linked the fortunes of experimental geneticists, who were wedded to a Newtonian methodology, to that of palaeontologists, who regarded themselves as the rightful heirs of nineteenth century natural historians such as Darwin. The key works here were Theodosius Dobzhansky's *Genetics and the Origin of Species* (1937) and George Gaylord Simpson's *Tempo and Mode in Evolution* (1944). Notwithstanding the title of his *magnum opus*, *The Origin of Species by Means of Natural Selection* (1859), Darwin himself had little that was intelligible to say about the genetic mechanisms responsible for the origin of new species, and hence hard-headed geneticists were inclined to write off evolution as woolly minded speculation. Moreover, by the first decades of the the twentieth century, Darwin's biggest supporters, his fellow natural historians, had come to be seen as the least professional of the life scientists, since their journals still published anecdotalist amateurs, who contributed little to the theoretical development of the field. Nevertheless, in a remarkable feat of scientific magnanimity, Dobzhansky, a population geneticist, initiated the synthesis by suppressing these clear methodological differences to show that natural historians provided evidence that was indeed relevant to the confirmation of genetic theories.[3] Simpson, a palaeontologist, used the time-honoured strategy of the 'just-so-story' to explain the adaptation of organisms to their environments, showing how the claims of geneticists and palaeontologists may plausibly reinforce each other without ever actually putting his hypothesis to the test.[4]

The contrast with the social sciences here could not be more striking. Psychology, perhaps, presents the most heroic case of failure to reconcile the interests of its practitioners working in 'artificial' and 'natural' settings, given that the field's leading methodologist in recent times, Donald Campbell (1916–96), had in principle effected such a reconciliation in his formulation of 'quasi-experimental' methods designed to approximate laboratory conditions 'non-obtrusively' in real life settings.[5] Yet, no one persuasively stepped into the role of Dobzhansky or Simpson to show how these methods could integrate, into a conceptually coherent synthesis, the substantive findings of psychologists working in otherwise opposed branches of the field. Instead, psychologists simply used Campbell's methods to support their own immediate research projects. Meanwhile, since Campbell first presented his hybrid methodology in the early 1960s, psychology has reached the disciplinary breaking point, as experimentalists and clinical practitioners now periodically threaten to go their separate ways.

One explanation for this marked difference in the fates of biology and psychology is that 'real' scientists possess a special mental faculty, traditionally called *intellectual intuition*, that enables them to penetrate a deeper order beneath the surface chaos of empirical observations. Certainly, this opinion has had a distinguished, if somewhat contested, pedigree in the history of philosophy, including Plato and Leibnitz among its defenders. Indeed, even biologists continue to marvel at the apparently unerring ability that physicists have to intuit perfect curves from otherwise unruly data points.[6] But an equally viable explanation for these mental achievements is that physicists are not as scrupulous as, say, psychologists in accounting for the data generated by a body of experimental work.[7] Since psychologists presume that their subject matter is quite complex and elusive, they do not pretend to have many clear intuitions about which data are worth keeping or throwing out when drawing some theoretically relevant inference. Consequently, they have been among the pioneers in the development of sophisticated 'meta-analytic' statistical techniques capable of integrating *all* the data from *all* the experiments.[8] Needless to say, these techniques produce a rather complicated overall empirical picture of psychological phenomena, one that resists simple theoretical formulations. Because physicists presume that they have a relatively clear understanding of their experimental situations, they have greater confidence in their own discretionary judgements of data. In addition, this difference in methodological attitudes between psychologists and physicists draws on divergent folk images of their competence as scientists, images that have themselves rarely been subject to empirical scrutiny. For example, while physicists are commonly seen as superior scientists, some of the most thoughtful and rigorous works on scientific methodology have been written by psychologists such as Campbell.

Some natural scientists have expressed scepticism at the ease with which different branches of their fields have synchronized their thinking. For example, contrary to the popular belief that the different branches of physics are independently converging upon a 'Grand Unified Theory', one physicist who deserted the fold for science journalism claims that there is collusion between particle physicists and cosmologists, in that the former have increasingly tried to come up with mathematical formulations that satisfy the theoretical expectations of the latter, all in the absence of any observational base or crucial experiment that could test these mutually reinforcing speculations.[9] Thus, while particle physics offers no direct evidence for a uniformly expanding universe after the Big Bang, such a view would nicely dovetail with cosmologists' beliefs, and hence particle physicists have placed mathematical constraints on their own theories that would allow such inflation to occur.

This raises the larger historical question of accountability in physics. While theories in the other sciences are routinely discounted if they are incompatible with the leading physical theories, it seems that physical theories need not be compatible with theories in the other sciences. At the end of the nineteenth century, the greatest physicist of his day, William Thomson, Lord Kelvin (1824–1907), declared that Darwinian evolution had to be false because thermodynamics did not allow the earth to be as old as evolution required. After this pronouncement, many scientifically minded biologists began to rethink their commitment to Darwin's view that nature operates by slow, steady changes. Indeed, this period witnessed a physics-induced revival of the periodic geological cataclysms postulated by the rival 'catastrophist' approach that was associated with Creationist attempts to read the Noachian Flood into the Earth's fossil record. Luckily (at least for the fate of Darwinism), physicists soon stumbled upon a refutation of Kelvin's chronology in their own bailiwick, once radioactivity was discovered as a source of heat that could have fuelled the Earth's core for the hundreds of millions of years needed for evolution.[10] Although today's fundamental physical theories postulate that the world is radically different at the extremes (the very big, the very small, the very old, etc.) from the way it appears at the 'middle' level of reality canvassed by the other sciences, few non-physicists have had the temerity to argue that physics is incompatible, or somehow out of step, with current trends in the rest of the sciences.[11] However, if one *wanted* to make such an argument, evidence could be sought by noticing the increased amounts being spent on particle accelerators that generate findings of little obvious cross-disciplinary relevance.

Finally, we must ask whether collusion in the various branches of a science, such as physics, somehow corrupts the entire scientific enterprise. At the very least, scientists can be charged with hyperbole in the import they assign to their agreements (which is no doubt useful in securing continued funding). A social scientist may appreciate the closeness with which elite theoretical physicists cooperate with each other today by imagining what it would be like for historians to agree on a general account of the evolution of society (no small feat in its own right), in which the evolutionarily most salient features of the earliest communities happened to be the very features that social psychologists have found to be most salient in their attempts to simulate small group processes in laboratory experiments. Too good to be true? Much depends on whether one can draw a line between fruitful collaboration and sinister collusion, and whether scientists turn out to fall on the right side of the line. It seems important to draw the line because science's authority as a reliable form of knowledge typically presupposes that the findings of its practitioners are more the result of *individual discovery* than *collective invention*. If discoveries converge upon a more general pattern of thought, then that must be the result of reality 'pulling' in that direction, and not of disciplinary norms 'pushing' scientists that way. But given that scientists so rarely break rank with disciplinary norms – and quickly close ranks against those who do – how can one tell whether convergence is being pushed or pulled?

Here we must turn to some other sociologically peculiar features of science. One is the sort of story that scientists tell about themselves and their colleagues in other scientific fields. Scientists first encounter this story in the opening chapters of their textbooks, which they then pass on to their students and the public, via science popularization. Depending on whether one is drawn to a physics or biology based model of the natural sciences, one can describe it as a version of the 'nebular hypothesis' of the universe's origins or an especially purpose laden version of organic evolution. (Ironically, each of these stories would be dismissed as obsolete accounts of physical and biological phenomena, though accepted as the accounts of the history of physics and biology.) Thus, science emerged from either the 'molten mass' or 'primordial soup' of philosophical speculation, gradually taking shape and dividing into functionally differentiated disciplines, each with its own proper domain of inquiry and methods, which together constitute a systematic understanding of reality that is slowly coming into focus as these disciplines capture the details of their domains. Obscured from this story are the large methodological, and perhaps even metaphysical, differences that still separate physics and biology, as mentioned earlier, although biologists routinely suffer in silence as the story officially has physics splitting off from philosophy nearly two centuries before biology. Occasionally a physicist, usually a Nobel Prize winner, will remind biologists of their subordinate status in science's grand narrative. A vivid case in point is the recent demotion of palaeontologists to the ranks of 'stamp collectors' by Nobel physicist Luis Alvarez, when they balked at his hypothesis that a meteor shower was responsible for the extinction of dinosaurs on Earth.[12]

Nevertheless, natural scientists are generally sheltered from experiencing any cross-disciplinary dissonance because the potted histories they encounter in their textbooks are more like the narratives recounted in science popularizations than in the works of professional historians of science. The latter typically accentuate the blind alleys, dirty deals, and strategic omissions that have enabled the history of science to appear seamless and progressive. Indeed, the most influential historian of science in recent memory, Thomas Kuhn, has gone so far as to justify this difference in the histories that scientists read and historians write on the grounds that, were fledgling scientists exposed to an unvarnished view of their past, they would be discouraged from the single-mindedness needed for working on highly specialized problems that hold little meaning outside their immediate research contexts.[13] Under the circumstances, it is not unreasonable to wonder whether Kuhn is more part of the problem than the solution to science's vexed role in society.[14] Nevertheless, his argument is far from unprecedented. We shall continually encounter versions in this book under the rubric of the *Double Truth* doctrine.

In contrast, students of social science are typically exposed to the history of their fields as part of the required curriculum. Often the people teaching these courses believe that the wrong research programmes have come to dominate their fields, and then only under very fortuitous circumstances that have little to do with the genuine validity of those programmes. Sometimes this state of affairs is traced to the permeability of the social science disciplines by larger societal concerns. After all, the first modern scientific association, the Royal Society, famously managed to thrive, in large part, because it explicitly prohibited such concerns from entering its deliberations. But at the same time, that was precisely what made the Royal Society an elite association, the repercussions of which we shall see shortly. In my own estimation, the injection of history into the social science curriculum has enabled those fields to aspire to a more common-sensical 'universal' form of knowledge than has been the case in the natural sciences for most of the twentieth century. The typical history of the social sciences contains a wider cross-section of social actors than the typical history of the natural sciences. Along with professionally certified social scientists, the history of a social science will routinely include politicians, policy makers, natural scientists, financiers, and even representatives of the primary and secondary school sectors.[15] In short, we have here *science in history* more than *history of science*.

If we return for a moment to the early days of the Royal Society, we see that the natural sciences' distinctive sense of focus is the product of self-censorship. Our chief witness is Thomas Hobbes (1588–1679). According to Hobbes, in a world where everyone is allowed to argue claims as they see fit, there will be no natural point of agreement. The imposition of closure on dispute thus becomes a political necessity, but one without any pretence to having resolved the dispute to everyone's satisfaction. These points were originally raised against Robert Boyle (1627–91), who wanted to restrict entry into the Royal Society to mutually recognized experts in the craft of experiment, among whom agreement could be easily reached on the nature and significance of empirical findings.[16] In this way, Boyle would pre-empt a Hobbesian 'war of all against all' at the level of discourse. However, from Hobbes's vantage point, what Boyle and his allies wanted to pass off as their superior insight, or 'credibility' as witnesses to nature, reflected nothing more than the mundane fact that similarly conditioned people will see things in similar ways. In the short term, Boyle won and Hobbes was excluded from the Royal Society. However, a more exact rendition is that Boyle and Hobbes have split the difference in the modern academy. Taking the craft of writing for professional journals as our benchmark, the natural sciences follow Boyle. Early in their professional training, students learn how to write for the journals in which they should publish. They do not submit an article for editoral scrutiny until they already believe that its chances of acceptance are high. Such mastery at self-censorship accounts for why natural science journals seem to maintain high standards despite having very high acceptance rates. At the level of the editorial forum, the natural sciences seem quite democratic, as most journals apply the same standards of critical judgement to the work submitted, regardless of the source. But a latter-day Hobbes would quickly observe that authors and editors converge so easily only because those who submit to such journals have been pre- and self-selected so as to minimize the possibility that a substantial divergence of opinion would ever reach the forum.

In contrast, professional training in the social sciences is less focused on journal writing, largely because there is less agreement over which journals one should write for. Consequently, editors of social science journals must often discipline and reject in public the sorts of utterances that would have been deleted by the prudent natural science author prior to submission. This leaves the overall impression that the low acceptance rates in social science journals is due just as much to a divergence of standards as to a surfeit of poorly crafted articles. Under the circumstances, it is natural to interpret editorial decisions as exercises of 'political' rather than strictly 'epistemic' authority. The appearance of politically motivated decisions, in turn, spurs the proliferation of 'alternative' journals where rejected authors can find editorial solace. Nevertheless, for all its fractiousness, the Hobbesian would argue that the social sciences at least enjoy the virtue of being open in its dealings. It remains to be seen whether the natural sciences genuinely succeed in sifting out a distinctly 'epistemic' dimension, or whether epistemology is simply the velvet glove cloaking the iron fist of academic politics.[17]

The profound difference between Boylean and Hobbesian sensibilities raises the following question. Does the culture of contestation that is so much more open in the social than the natural sciences enliven or trivialize knowledge claims? And what does the answer tell us about the nature of scientific knowledge? While virtually every philosopher and scientist has endorsed some version of the idea that criticism is the lifeblood of epistemic growth, most of them have recoiled from the promiscuous pursuit of criticism. The officially expressed fear is that inchoate or controversial research programmes may be prematurely terminated if they fail to answer criticisms when they are lodged. Even if the criticisms miss their target, they may leave enough doubts to make it that much harder for the targeted programme to develop. Moreover, if the activity of lodging criticisms is itself too highly valued, then inquirers will lose all incentive to develop their own knowledge claims beyond a certain point. For these reasons, philosophers and scientists have tried to come up with ways of protecting certain kinds of knowledge claims from immediate attack. Sometimes they appeal to logic, sometimes to history, and, increasingly, to expertise, but the net effect is to defer the critic's access to the forum. At a practical level, this attitude wreaks havoc on the scholarly refereeing system. Genuinely probing referees' reports often go unheeded (let alone unappreciated) because scholarly authors are encouraged to work out their arguments with such thoroughness prior to submission that they are psychologically ill-disposed to any response that would have them rethink major portions of their position. In this way, the whole point of criticism is routinely defeated.

The rhetorical intuitions informing science's love–hate relationship with criticism merit extended examination. In part, criticism is loathed because it is seen as playing a destructive rather than a creative role in thought. At most, it is seen as a selection mechanism. Philosophers prefer theories that are reasonably developed before being subjected to criticism, and they regard theories that receive most of their elaboration in the face of criticism as having been ill-conceived or *ad hoc*. However, history throws up some rather embarrassing counterexamples. After all, only half of Darwin's *The Origin of Species* remained intact after its first dozen years of publication. Perhaps a big part of science's mystique, then, lies in its dialectical encounters being portrayed as do-or-die struggles that occur relatively rarely because of the magnitude of the stakes. This would certainly explain the extent to which a theory must be developed before being brought to the forum. Conversely, respect for science may conceivably diminish if too many of its knowledge claims are too frequently contested, as is the case in the social sciences. We shall probably be in a position to test this hypothesis in the near future, given the proliferation of electronic networks in *both* the social sciences and natural sciences, whose debates cut across – and often against – more 'respectable' print forums.[18]

In conclusion, there are at least three levels at which the language of science functions to establish its authority in society. They correspond conveniently to the traditional levels of linguistic analysis: *syntactic, semantic,* and *lexical. Syntactically,* scientific discourse displays modes of expression, even entire narratives, that enable collective remembering and forgetting to occur across a variety of disciplines that would otherwise have little in common. This is especially important in terms of scientists presenting a united front of overall progress to a sceptical public. *Semantically,* the technical discourse of particular sciences enables a map of knowledge to be drawn which sets the boundaries of expertise. In that sense, scientific language is ready-made to express intellectual property claims. Any examination of the refereeing practices of 'peer-reviewed' journals bears out this point.[19] Finally, at the *lexical* level, scientists, in their day-to-day interactions, typically address each other using unexceptional language that is punctuated by specific technical terms that have no ordinary correlates. Thus, the lexical level plays against the semantic and syntactic ones, since typically the mundane character of life in the laboratory needs to be masked in order for the products of its activities to be regarded as genuine contributions to knowledge.[20] Inaccessibility confers privilege. As it turns out, when scientists are interrogated on their practices, their first line of defence tends to be in the potted syntactic mode. However, the diligent inquirer can get the scientist past this verbal facade to the semantic and lexical levels, whereby science starts to look like something encountered in other walks of life.[21] If one needed a 'methodological' proof of the relationship of critical scrutiny and democracy, it is the success of such linguistic probing.

Notes

1 Dewey (1908: ch. VI). This example, in turn, served as the paradigm case of the deductive-nomological model of scientific explanation in the logical positivist classic, Hempel (1965: 335–8).
2 Gould (1989).
3 Ceccarelli (1995).
4 Journet (1995).
5 Campbell and Stanley (1966).
6 Wolpert (1992: 96–8).
7 Hedges (1987).
8 On meta-analysis, see Shadish and Fuller (1993: 214–61).
9 Lindley (1993: ch. 6).
10 Lindley (1993: ch. 1).
11 In part out of dissatisfaction with the autonomous character of recent physics research, some efforts have been made to embed fundamental physics in an overall evolutionary picture of the universe as a 'self-organizing system'. Much of this work is indebted to the thermo-dynamicist Ilya Prigogine. See Hooker (1987).
12 For an astonishingly gracious response, see Gould (1989: 280–81).
13 Kuhn (1970: 32, 167); also Brush (1975).
14 Fuller (1998).
15 Goodson (1988).
16 Shapin and Schaffer (1985)
17 The social sciences that have tried the *hardest* to emulate the natural sciences can be made especially vulnerable to the charge that their politics is barely disguised. One notorious experiment was conducted on the 'hardest' end of psychology, neurophysiology, showing that previously accepted articles were rejected by the journals that had published them, once they were resubmitted by authors claiming to hail from low status universities. See Peters and Ceci (1982).
18 For some heated exchanges over whether the electronic medium should perfect or undermine the peer review process and, in either case, how, see Kling (1995).
19 Chubin and Hackett (1990).
20 Knorr-Cetina (1981) is especially good on this point.
21 Gilbert and Mulkay (1984).

3

'Science', 'Scientific', 'Scientist': Some Exercises in Conceptual Analysis

Science

The word *science* is semantically more complex than it first appears. For a start, we need to distinguish between 'science' as an abstract and a concrete noun: that is, the difference between what it means for something to be a science and the content of a particular science. So, what does it mean for something to be a science? We can give either a *substantive* or a *functional* answer to this question, which roughly corresponds to a philosophical and a sociological definition of science, respectively. Philosophers tend to focus on features that are supposedly inherent to a knowledge practice, typically its mode of operation or 'method', whereas sociologists stress the role that the knowledge practice plays in relation to other social practices. The sociological definition usefully complements the philosophical one, since, as we have already seen, the specific disciplines grouped together as 'sciences' bear little resemblance to each other in their day-to-day conduct. Nevertheless, it may be that these rather disparate disciplines serve a similar function in the larger society, something the sociological definition begins to come to grips with. In contrast, philosophers have had to abstract heroically from these disciplines to arrive at a 'method' they might all share. Unfortunately, the results are so removed from the actual scientific practice that only the professional theorists and methodologists in those disciplines – that is, the scientists whose own work most resembles that of philosophers – have seen the relevance of such an abstract characterization of science. Of course, this is not to deny the relevance of this philosophical discourse to the potted syntactic mode discussed at the end of the last chapter, through which science presents its public face.

Interestingly, although philosophers and sociologists seem to look at science from quite different angles, their definitions ultimately gravitate towards two polar ideologies, which can be called *Enlightenment* and *Positivist*, after two self-styled pro-science Western intellectual movements that originally flourished in the eighteenth and nineteenth centuries. For our purposes, the two movements can be made to stand for two general trends in the history of science. On the one hand, the Enlightenment envisions what it calls 'science' as a mentality that potentially pervades all of society and hence cannot be restricted to the activities of an elite group. In this respect, science can be seen on a par with other secularizing forces such as Protestantism and capitalism. On the other hand, Positivism presupposes that science is practised primarily (or perhaps ideally) by academic specialists, professional 'scientists', who may in turn administer to the larger society as civil servants or policy analysts. Both movements are committed to *universality* as a feature of scientific knowledge which, regardless of its origins, makes it knowledge for *everyone*. But whereas Enlightenment thinkers see universality as the long term consequence of people criticizing each other's dogmatic attitudes, their Positivist counterparts locate universality at the outset of inquiry, more specifically in the disciplined mental attitude of professional inquirers. An Enlightenment thinker would find the purpose of science defeated if, after a period of intense critical scrutiny, a set of doctrines surviving such scrutiny became the indubitable foundations for knowledge, which in turn defined the parameters within which subsequent critical inquiry would be contained. Yet, this is precisely what the Positivist proposes. It was not by accident that Positivism's founder, Auguste Comte (1798–1857), saw in science's universalist aspirations a natural successor to the Roman Catholic Church. In philosophical terms, the Enlightenment's interest in strong tests to falsify established beliefs is countered by Positivism's concern with reconstructing knowledge on a reliable body of data and logic,

	Philosophical substance	Sociological function	The opposite of science
Enlightenment	Falsifiability	Delegitimation	Unquestioned prejudice
Positivist	Verifiability	Legitimation	Unruly opinion

Figure 3.1 Enlightenment and Positivism.

which can then be used to bring consensus to society at large. If one fears the inertia of mindlessly reproduced tradition, the other fears the chaos of disordered thought. These differences are summarized in Figure 3.1.

But, of course, 'science' is also, and perhaps more recognizably, a concrete noun, a specific set of practices whose unique access to reality serves as the standard against which other practices (and their practitioners) can be evaluated. The best way to follow the history of science in this sense is by identifying, across cultures and centuries, the disciplines that are taken to exemplify the virtue 'science', or its cognate term. In the West, until roughly the mid-nineteenth century, this history coincided with the history of philosophy, especially that of *natural philosophy*. However, philosophy and science went their separate ways once 'scientist' was coined as the name of a specific profession. Before turning to that development, consider the representation in Figure 3.2 of the history of Western science.

Crucial to understanding the history of 'science' as a concrete noun is knowing the sort of practices that have counted as the opposite of science, that is, *anti-science*. Since any social practice of some

	Abstract virtue	Concrete exemplar	Concrete opposite
Ancient Greek	Episteme	Geometry	Rhetoric
Medieval Latin	Scientia	Theology	Magic
Nineteenth-Century German	Wissenschaft	History	Metaphysics
Twentieth-Century English	Science	Physics	Common sense

Figure 3.2 The history of Western science.

longevity can reasonably lay claim to having reliable access to reality, societies have needed ways of discriminating better and worse sorts of access. For example, simply knowing that the ancient Greeks regarded geometry as the exemplar of *episteme* is not very illuminating until we learn that rhetoric epitomized anti-science for them. For the Greek philosophers Plato (428–348BC) and Aristotle (384–322BC), rhetoric was a bag of verbal tricks whose success could not be guaranteed or even explained very well, as it seemed to elude the norms of logical reasoning.[1] By contrast, geometry earned its scientific status because it provides proofs that demonstrate exactly how a conclusion follows from a set of premises by the application of a series of simple and explicit rules. Much of this geometric sensibility was retained once the exemplar shifted to theology in the Middle Ages. However, because even the most devout theologian could not grant the conclusiveness of proofs for the existence of God, it became sufficient to distinguish between beliefs that are justified, albeit inconclusively, from superstitious beliefs based solely on anecdote, rumour, or alleged personal powers. Thus, the Greek aim of logical closure was replaced with an emphasis on the public character of knowledge, which in turn represented the theologian's stewardship over God's Creation. Opposed to this sensibility was knowledge of magic, the reliability of which could not be tested because of its inherently esoteric nature. Magicians typically traced their powers to the special agreements they have struck with supernatural entities that circumvent the normal order of things and, at least indirectly, threaten to undermine a unified conception of Creation.

By the time we enter the world of *Wissenschaft*, all hope of arriving at universal claims to knowledge that command intuitive assent has disappeared. The image of knowledge *production* truly came into its own in the nineteenth century, as insight and wit were replaced by hard work applied to the transformation of raw materials: first documents in the archives; then specimens in the field; and finally artifacts in the laboratory. The *seminar* emerged as the site for subsuming education under research (as opposed to the medieval practice of the *lecture*, which subsumed in reverse by reducing research to textbook commentary). Not surprisingly, the proponents of this quintessentially Positivistic vision regarded their Enlightenment predecessors as mischievous metaphysicians.

It may seem strange to find the discipline of history as the exemplar of science in this context, given that the seventeenth century had already witnessed the rise of organizations like the Royal Society, explicitly designed to promote the experimental sciences as we understand them today. Nevertheless, laboratory based inquiry continued to carry the stigma of the magical arts until the second half of the nineteenth century. Indeed, the status of most experimental science before that time was comparable to that of computer programming today: a field whose innovations are most likely to come from hackers whose exploits are 'legendary' in all senses of that word (consider the powers attributed to computer viruses) and apparently governed by such unserious motives as fun and profit. For their part, proper computer scientists primarily codify and certify the hacker inspired developments. More generally, the association of science with the official codification and certification of knowledge came about with the renovation of the national university systems of Europe, canonically beginning with the founding of the University of Berlin in 1810 by Wilhelm von Humboldt (1767–1835). Henceforth, the universities became the cornerstone of the modern nation state. The practitioners of science were civil servants entrusted with consolidating the national knowledge base by preserving only those claims that survived critical scrutiny. The model of criticism was the juridical interrogation of documents to establish who was entitled to what. Under the circumstances, the archetype of anti-science was a practice whose conclusions could not be settled by appeals to evidence. Kant, his own writings laden with metaphors drawn from the courtroom, showed that metaphysics has just this objectionable characteristic in its attempt to seek indubitable truths at a level of reality that transcends empirical inquiry.

Today's understanding of science is distinguished by two additional features. First, science has shed its aristocratic class prejudices against manual labour and commercial gain, which from the mid-seventeenth century to the mid-nineteenth century had prevented those factory like institutions, laboratories, from being housed on university grounds. This development is, in part, a natural result of the enrolment of ever larger segments of the citizenry into civil and military service functions and, in part, a reflection of the incursion of capitalism into such a resolutely non-economic sector of society as the academy. Secondly, the legitimatizing goals of science have shifted from explicit service to the state to service to science itself; or at least one now says that the goals of the state cannot be properly served until those of science are first served. Such is the operational definition of 'science for its own sake'. Indeed, the 'universality' of science has come to be identified, at least in the popular imagination, with just this attitude, rather than the widespread distribution of scientific knowledge as such. In practical terms, research is nowadays justified as somehow feeding back into teaching, so as to assure students that they are receiving an education that will enable them to deal with a rapidly changing world. Long gone are the days when scientific knowledge actually *stabilized* the society in which the knowledge was produced.[2] Rather, one now routinely expects the fruits of scientific research to be counterintuitive, if not completely beyond the understanding of the untutored lay person. Science's open defiance of common-sense probably reached its peak in the late 1920s, shortly after the twofold revolution in relativity and quantum physics. This defiance was even canonized as a philosophical conundrum by Arthur Eddington (1882–1944) as the 'two tables paradox', which implied that people simply had to learn to accept that a table is *both* a hard, wooden object and a swarm of atoms moving around in otherwise empty space.[3]

Scientific

The next word to be subject to semantic scrutiny is *scientific*, which may have any of three meanings, each easily identified by a synonym:

1 *science's* – a property of science, as in the 'scientific method';
2 *scientized* – an application of science, as in 'scientific agriculture';
3 *scientistic* – an imitation of science, as in 'scientific sociology'.

The three synonyms are arranged according to their (increasing) distance from the actual conduct of scientific inquiry. In this respect, the nuance in meaning separating 2 and 3 is especially important, as it reflects the difference between scientists colonizing domains they previously had not inhabited (2) and the inhabitants of those domains remaking themselves in order to attract the approval of scientists (3). Philosophers have traditionally papered over this difference in the direction of cross-disciplinary exchange by the feat of heroic abstraction known as *reductionism*, which refers to any attempt to extend the rule of science beyond its normal disciplinary confines, regardless of who originates the move. For example, today's 'equilibrium' models of the economy, which stress the need to maintain a balance between supply and demand, look like something out of nineteenth-century accounts of energy conservation and expenditure. Is this a case of physicists trying to tell economists what to do or of economists borrowing physics to tell each other what to do? It turns out that an adverse job market has muddled the distinction, as people trained in physics (or theoretically based engineering) have actually migrated to economics and successfully converted their oversubscribed skills into a revolutionary new expertise.[4]

Minimally, a domain is scientifically 'reduced' once an acknowledged method of science has been imported. But, of course, the substantive beliefs of a science may be imported as well, as when philosophy takes the latest science as the foundation of, or at least ultimate constraint on, its speculations. Some cases in point are to suppose that the nature of the mind can be solved by mapping the brain; that the secret to the good society can be unravelled by articulating the genetic make-up of humans; or that questions of ultimate reality can be settled by physicists discovering fundamental particles and forces.[5] These three examples share two interesting features. First, the implementation of the reductionist programme involves the introduction of new techniques for acquiring and expressing knowledge, which in turn limit the sorts of people who can participate in them. Secondly, the resources required for providing reductionist answers greatly exceed what had been needed for pursuing these questions in their 'pre-reduced' state. It is almost as if financial commitment were doing the work that in previous generations had been done by the provision of evidence: the more we spend on a research programme, the less we can imagine that it could be misguided.

Painting on a broader conceptual canvas, we can map the semantics of the 'scientific' in terms of whether the influence of science is concentrated or dispersed in society at large. Where the influence is concentrated, the interface between science and society can be characterized as a *site*, and where the influence is dispersed, the interface is a *process*. From a social scientific standpoint, sites are the objects of anthropological study, processes of sociohistorical study. The result is the 'interpenetration' of science and society in

	Science socialized	*Society scientized*
Science/society as site	A Science reproduces social institutions and general social tendencies	B Society reaches its full potential in science
Science/society as process	C Science becomes diffuse as it is popularized	D Society becomes standardized as it comes under the rule of science

Figure 3.3   The interpenetration of science and society.

Figure 3.3. In Chapter 4, I shall reveal a previously unreleased anthropological inventory of science, which will address issues related to A and B. So, for now, let us make do with some remarks on the countervailing processes of science's social influence, that is, C and D in Figure 3.3.

In the case of C, despite the Enlightenment's interest in spreading the critical cast of the scientific mind across society, it is just this mind-set that is most likely to drop out as scientific ideas enter general circulation. When noticed at all, science tends to be received uncritically as dogma.[6] Public interest in science is typically piqued by tabloid newspaper reports of medical breakthroughs and freak occurrences in nature, and not by such relatively arcane matters as the 'selfish gene' or 'black holes', unless, that is, they are seen as assimilable to more accessible topics (e.g. genetically based defects in prospective offspring). However, this lack of critical engagement with science has seemed to serve science well, at least if one thinks of science's continued survival as an end in itself. Knowledge and interest can interact in peculiar ways. (Here one thinks of how the stability of democratic regimes depends on the bulk of the population failing to participate in the political process, either out of relative contentment or sheer indifference.) It is plainly fallacious to suppose that, just because science enjoys widespread public support with relatively few people holding reliable beliefs about it, support would increase were people to have more in-depth knowledge of science. If sociologists get hold of them, the people may be outraged; if professional scientists get hold of them, they may simply be bored. Strange as it may seem, much like the workings of government in large democratic regimes, science may be popular *precisely* because it is misunderstood. Thus, a movement genuinely devoted to the 'public understanding of science' may have some rather unintended consequences for the future of science.

Generally speaking, practising scientists are only a small fraction of those who contribute to any socially acceptable definition of science. Among the other contributors are practitioners in other disciplines (especially the social sciences), who model their own fields on the scientific exemplars of their day; science policy makers; and, especially, science popularizers, including those who read Buddhism into the breakdown of causation at the quantum level of physical reality. It is easy to conclude that these hangers-on simply do not understand what they are talking about. However, were the scientific community to disown them so brusquely, science would quickly lose its esteemed social standing. After all, why would democratic governments want to invest billions of dollars on activities from which only a few directly benefit and to which the rest can hardly relate? From a sociological standpoint, all of the misbegotten metaphors and half-understandings of science that infiltrate the popular imagination are what enables a broad spectrum of people to project their own experiences and traditions onto the otherwise elite and alien world of scientific research. Perhaps not surprisingly, scientists openly object to this dilution of their message only once the public feels sufficiently empowered by its 'understanding' to want to take science policy into their own hands.

In the case of D, the principal way in which society comes under the rule of science is through the *naturalization* of everyday understandings of reality. This process is most recognizable as the alleged continuity between animal instinct, common sense, and the scientific method as degrees of 'cognitive engagement' with, or 'environmental adaptation' to, the natural world. This fusion of terms is often grounded in the Darwinian notion that precedents for most of the defining properties of *Homo sapiens* can be found, at least in nascent form, throughout the animal kingdom. For example, 'cognition' turns out to be perception that has been evolutionarily enhanced by memory and foresight. But in the next breath, one makes it quite clear that 'scientific knowledge' is probably the best mode of adaptation that our species – perhaps any species – has evolved. Together, these two views end up licensing the conclusion that the pursuit of science is a natural extension of people's innate

'curiosity', or some such animal tendency, and that palpably anti-
scientific trends such as religious fundamentalism or political
authoritarianism prevent us from realizing our full potential.

Among the long-term institutional consequences of this position
has been the introduction of 'scientific' criteria – typically inspired
by physics – to evaluate the full range of human adaptive skills that
naturalists generically lump together under the rubric of 'cognition'
or 'intelligence'. The most blatant example of this tendency must
be Jean Piaget's (1896–1980) influential model of child development, whereby the cognitive trajectory from infancy to adolescence
supposedly recapitulates the past 2000 years of the history of
Western physical science. Yet, as we saw in Chapter 2, even
someone as democratically inclined as Dewey held related views.
Admittedly, neither Piaget nor Dewey had much training in
physics, but several of the early proponents of intelligence testing,
and cognitive psychology more generally, did. For them it was quite
natural to envisage the notebooks of a great physicist like Benjamin
Franklin or Michael Faraday as containing self-elicited protocols of
their thought processes, making them exceptionally good witnesses
to mental events that everyone else experiences unconsciously.[7]
Given how easily the past is forgotten, one could predict that within
50 years someone would turn this development on its head by
looking to concept acquisition in children as a model of how novices
acquire the basic principles and techniques of a science.[8]

It may seem liberal to say that nobody is held back from attaining the epistemic respectability of a scientist. Yet, such hopeful
expressions were routinely translated into strategies for turning
everyone into a scientist, at least before they were turned into anything else. Thus, for most of the twentieth century, the 'formal
reasoning' ability of students has been gauged by their success at
constructing and manipulating the simultaneous equations needed
to solve watered-down versions of 'work problems' in classical
mechanics.[9] Failure to perform adequately on such tests seriously
hampered career choice and mobility, regardless of how tangential
the skills measured by those tests were to actual employment
prospects.[10] Thus, the 'democratization' of educational institutions
refers to nothing more than the fact that increasing numbers of
people undergo the same sets of standardized examinations before
being awarded degrees and jobs. To be sure, these reforms have
been 'democratic' in the sense of subordinating everyone to a

common standard of achievement, but at the same time, they have effectively removed alternative paths of advancement, especially such experience based ones as working one's way up from the stockroom.[11] While the rhetoric of 'cognitivism' that has accompanied this development is designed to distance knowledge-ability from sociability, it is only once some aspect of human psychology is infused with a 'cognitive dimension' that a clear license is given for others to come between your body and your soul by introducing training programs and performance standards. The question that remains to be asked is *should* people have to prove themselves decent little physicists before they are permitted to pursue the line of work they really want or society really needs?

Scientist

Although 'science' and cognate terms can be found in most Indo–European languages, 'scientist' does not appear until well into the nineteenth century. The significance of this fact should not be underestimated. It is one thing to think of the organized pursuit of knowledge as something that can be analysed independently of other social practices; it is quite another to think of its pursuit as a full-time job, a profession that requires specialist credentials. For example, we can regard the bodily functions as a field of study – call it 'physiology' – without thereby concluding that only 'physiologists' really know how to breathe and eat, with the rest of humanity merely improvising those bodily functions to the best of their meagre abilities. More generally, the possibility of a 'scientist' suggests that only certain people have really applied their minds to fathoming specific domains of reality. Through their training and commitment, these people have supposedly acquired intellectual skills that make them exemplars to whom other members of society should defer when seeking insight into these domains. The model for this development is clearly the priesthood, whereby a society comes to accept the idea that its members cannot properly deal with their souls without third party mediation. An example better suited to our secular times is the widespread belief that one should consult a medical doctor before judging the state of one's health. After all, before medicine adopted the quantitative methods of the physical sciences, physicians actually had to *persuade* potential patients of their prowess in healing and caring.[12]

Over the past 150 years, scientists have colonized (typically without popular consent) various features of reality to which the rest of society had been previously accorded more-or-less direct access. A good way to see this is by noting the marked drop in the contributions of 'amateurs' to scientific journals during this period. The prospect that someone without the right academic accreditation (and, in most cases, affiliation) could make a formal contribution to science is nowadays deeply problematic, in a way it would not have been even earlier in the twentieth century. The insidious flipside of this tendency is that if someone possesses the proper credentials, their acuteness of reasoning is taken for granted. In other words, the 'laws of thought' are *not* treated like civil laws, whereby police officers, judges, and lawyers are just as accountable as ordinary citizens to the laws. However, when experts are subjected to the level of scrutiny that lay people normally encounter, their performance is often not too impressive.[13] It would seem, then, that standards of knowing invite a double standard. What count as infractions and signs of a debased cognitive status when committed by a non-adept in the sciences may be excused and even regarded as marks of creativity and genius when committed by a keeper of the standard, someone professionally qualified to 'know better'. Often a mysterious expression like 'tacit knowledge' is invoked to license the qualified knower's discretionary actions, and it is currently popular to say that truly intelligent behaviour cannot be reduced to rule-following.[14] Nevertheless, it is striking just how readily those rules are invoked whenever a novice or stranger needs to be set straight.

The emergence of the 'scientist' as a fixed social role takes us light-years, conceptually, from what both the Greek philosophers and the founders of Royal Society would have recognized as the social conditions for the pursuit of science. For them *leisure* was the sole necessary condition for sustained reflections out of which contributions to knowledge may emerge. Only in a state of leisure would there be no worry about one's reflections either unwittingly jeopardizing or unfairly promoting one's own welfare. We can already begin to understand the unique social arrangements that were needed to breed this sensibility. The elites who enjoyed the requisite leisure had to be of roughly equivalent status and power, without being preoccupied with outdoing each other in materialistic terms (which would incline them to deploy their knowledge purely to their own advantage). The Greeks clearly inhabited a pre-capitalist culture whose sense of 'economy' focused on household maintenance, not unbounded growth. For its part, the early Royal Society was largely a gentlemen's club in which personal tact was considered a component of technical prowess.

The historical transition from Enlightenment to Positivism as the dominant ideology of science corresponds roughly to the Industrial Revolution in Europe. Because the Enlightenment essentially saw science as the human faculty of reason writ large, it could conceive of payment for new scientific knowledge only in terms of *prizes*, and not salaries or even grants. Since any scientific problem was thought to be solvable by anyone who applied their mind to it, the relevant mental application would seem not to require any special economic conditions other than leisure. Thus, it made sense to conceive of the pursuit of science very much on the Greek model, as a contest to reach the finish line first and capture the prize. However, in the nineteenth century, this image of scientific inquiry rapidly broke down as a result of two convergent tendencies: an industrial 'push' and an academic 'pull'.

The first was the realization that systematically applying mechanical and chemical principles could markedly improve industrial productivity and hence one's position in the marketplace. Industrialists were therefore motivated to maintain the rate of technological innovation by training and employing potential inventors who would be entirely focused on inventing solutions to technical problems that would then be exclusively claimed by the industrial employer. Here we see the first stirrings of the idea of scientific knowledge as *intellectual property*, which implies, among other things, that the knowledge in question is directly available to the user only at a cost. Typically, this development is masked by the eagerness with which industry markets new products so as to encourage as many consumers as possible to purchase them. However, we should not confuse a 'hard sell' with free access.

In response to this general tendency, the universities, under the leadership of William Whewell (1794–1866), developed a complementary strategy. Whewell, Master of Trinity College Cambridge, was both a confirmed Anglican priest and the holder of a chair in mineralogy. His self-appointed task was to retell the history of science so that inventors such as James Watt (1736–1819) of steam engine fame were portrayed as having 'implicitly' mastered bodies of theoretical knowledge, which made them beneficiaries of an intellectual tradition whose guardians were to be found in the universities. This intellectual tradition consisted of the gradual revelation of the order that the Creator imposed on nature. Its cornerstone was Newtonian mechanics, which had been developed by a devout professor of mathematics in his spare time without the benefit of an external grant. Thus, links were forged between university culture and the mechanics and chemists who were proving useful to industry. In practical terms, Whewell's strategy enabled the universities to argue that it was possible to rationalize the process of inventiveness by having people matriculate in the underlying principles of physical reality, something that past inventors had only half-mastered. By successfully introducing 'scientist' into English parlance in the 1830s to cover the newly professionalized pursuit of science, Whewell had ensured that the universities would become arbiters of genuine inventiveness, that is, providers of theoretically respectable explanations for why inventions turn out to be sources of industrial innovation.[15] Philosophers have canonized Whewell's feat as the logic of *justification*, in contrast to the original context of *discovery*, which is commonly believed to have no logic at all.[16]

Notes

1 The debate over the relationship between science and rhetoric continues. See Gross and Keith (1996).
2 Beck (1992).
3 For an explication and critique of Eddington, see Stebbing (1937). She traces scientific contempt for common sense back to Newton's *Opticks* (1703). For an incisive examination of latter-day scientific challenges to common sense, see Midgley (1992).
4 For stories both of physicists migrating to economics and of economists borrowing physics to tell each other what to do, see Mirowski (1989), a historical indictment of his field's unreflective scientism.
5 A good survey of these forms of reductionism is Sorell (1991).
6 Moreover, this point applies equally to scientists outside a given speciality as to non-scientists more generally. To fathom the former, the reader is referred to the lengthening and somewhat mystifying literature on 'trust' in contemporary sociology. For a critique, see Fuller (1993b: 292–4).
7 I am alluding here to the sources for the early models of cognitive processing proposed by Otto Seltz and Karl Duncker in the 1920s, as well

as the reminiscences of the Gestalt psychologist Wolfgang Koehler, about the influence that his old physics professor, Max Planck, exerted on his thought. A good detailed history of the first fifty years of experimental cognitive psychology – that is, until just before the computer revolution – is Humphrey (1951).

8 The predicted person turned out to be the failed physicist Thomas Kuhn (1977: 293–319).

9 This way of testing formal reasoning ability can be traced back at least to the French founder of intelligence testing, Alfred Binet, and through his American followers Lewis Terman and David Wechsler. As Sternberg (1990: 81) observes, there has been a tendency to apply the test to younger children. Work problems originally given to 14-year-olds, are now given to 6-year-olds.

10 While there has always been a minority report against this tendency in educational psychology, the principled denial of a unified sense of 'knowing' – nowadays dubbed the 'multiple intelligences' thesis – began to command its current levels of research funding and media attention only once big business started to wonder aloud whether the standards of knowing and reasoning enforced by educators for most of this century were capable of adapting to capitalism's quickly changing competitive environment.

11 Ringer (1979: 27–9).

12 Leach (1996). The story is somewhat more complicated, since the inspiration for medicine's change in this direction came just as much from a statistically orientated social science as an experimentally oriented natual science. See Matthews (1995).

13 An analysis of the full range of psychology experiments comparing lay and expert performance on a variety of reasoning tasks is provided in Fuller (1993a: 106ff.). The general conclusion is that specializing in a content area does not necessarily increase one's powers of deductive or inductive reasoning.

14 Collins (1991).

15 Yeo (1993). Concerning Whewell's pivotal role in defining the scientist's role, it is worth noting the etymological roots of 'theory' in *theos* ('god' in Greek).

16 The *locus classicus* for this sentiment is Popper (1959), but it remains widespread even today.

4

Science as Superstition: A Lost Martian Chronicle

While researching a book on Thomas Kuhn in the Harvard University archives in May 1993, I stumbled upon a manuscript, *The Martian Ultraviolet Paper on that Distinctly Human Superstition Called 'Science'*.[1] It seems that this report was part of an omnibus survey of Earthly devotional rituals. The Martian anthropologists wanted to determine the functions – both real and imagined – served by these rituals. But how to go about it? In what follows, I paraphrase the contents of the report, occasionally inserting my own comments in parentheses. Apparently, the Martians intend(ed?) to intervene unobtrusively in our science policy forums to correct the 'errors' catalogued in this report. Since the report was designed exclusively for Martian consumption, it is rather brusque in dealing with matters that we tend to treat with considerable respect. Reader beware!

The first thing our Martians realize is that 'science' refers more to an ideal form of Earthly inquiry than the way inquiry is normally conducted. Ideally, the scientist is concerned with the difference that the truth or falsity of a hypothesis makes to understanding why something happens the way it does. In practice, the ideal boils down to conducting a test by experimental means, whereby an 'experiment' is a strategically made observation, one that often involves specially crafted machinery that focuses the scientist's mind on only the relevant features of the experimental situation. The ideal is most closely approximated in a highly controlled laboratory setting, which has somehow been deemed representative of a significant aspect of reality. The history of physics after the seventeenth century and of chemistry after the eighteenth century best match the ideal, but even then only if one allows for a certain generosity of spirit.

After all, our Martians realize that they would be open to charges of tactlessness if they dared to ask exactly how physicists know that their experiments have significance that goes beyond the immediate research facility or, for that matter, their research programme. (Nevertheless, they cannot be blamed for noticing that physics is often taken to be the 'foundational' science upon which the other sciences build, and is even sometimes thought to have provided definitive answers to questions first posed by the pre-Socratic Greek philosophers 2500 years earlier, despite the fact that most of those Greeks would have regarded experimental physics research as too far removed from 'nature' to be taken seriously as a valid source of knowledge of reality.[2]) While this point flags the peculiar relationship that science in its idealized sense has to the actual history of science, it should not prevent the Martians from observing that most biological, and even social, scientists aspire to and, in some cases, simulate the ideal of 'science'. However, once the Martians have mastered the subtleties behind the Earthly definition of science, how should they set out to get at the social functions that this quasi-fictional entity has for humans? As we shall see, after considering an array of options, they decide on a reflexive social epistemology, that is, they apply the scientists' own standards of rationality to what the scientists say and do.

The first possible strategy is to arrive disguised as a member of a group that is essential to reproducing the social order of science but traditionally marginal to its power structure. Depending on the exact criteria adopted, women, ethnic minorities, postdoctoral fellows and technical support staff would fall into this category. Not only would this disguise ensure anonymous treatment and an unselfconscious attitude on the part of those who wield power in science, but it would also enable the Martian to adopt the perspective, or *standpoint*, of someone who understands the system from the inside yet lacks a vested interest in the system's perpetuation under its current regime. Such a person would be especially well disposed to tell the difference between the merely habitual or forced and the genuinely desirable features of scientific activity.[3] (We shall exploit this interpretative strategy ourselves in Chapter 6, when looking at Western science from Japanese eyes.)

But on second thought, our Martian travellers decide on a persona less prone to render the natives internally divisive and alienated. If Earthly devotion to science can be depicted as something that a well adjusted Martian might be inclined to do under the right circumstances, then humans may turn out to be much saner than they seem. Perhaps, then, science should be studied as if it were any other social practice in which humans engage. In that case, the anthropologists would not need to strain to translate such mysterious terms as 'objectivity' and 'rationality'. However, additional reflection leads the Martians to judge this strategy equally wanting, because humans – not least scientists themselves – normally incorporate a large element of the exotic in their image of science. For the well meaning Martian to make Earthly devotion to science seem to be an extension of common sense and everyday life would be to miss much of the point and fervour attached to these rituals. After all, science is unique in the resources and respect that are voluntarily concentrated on a few 'experts' by the many who have never ventured through the doors of a laboratory, and hence know science, at best, only through what are widely regarded as its 'effects'.

The Martians place particular emphasis on this last point. At the level of personal experience, it may be rational for professional scientists to believe in science, but less so for the public, given that their encounters with science are restricted largely to its purported 'applications', be they medicines, machines or mathematics classes. Here religion provides a useful point of comparison: clerical authority is routinely complemented with doctrinal training for the faithful, which has periodically resulted in grass roots challenges to that authority, perhaps most notably in the Protestant Reformation of sixteenth century Europe. In contrast, although people receive enough technical training to operate machines, administer medicine and use calculators, basic science education is not sufficiently pervasive and coherent to lay the foundations for a Reformation-like movement 'from below' to develop against the scientific establishment. Rather, the situation is more like the Catholic Mass, in which competence as a worshipper does not extend to being qualified for assuming the priest's role as the Mass's official celebrant. Whereas critics of religious orthodoxy have generally tried to reclaim what they regard as the religion's original meaning, critics of the scientific orthodoxy have often wanted to make a total break with science, thereby reflecting their alienation from its mode of thought. There are many more 'ascientists' (compare 'atheists') than scientific heretics.[4] As for the attitudes of scientists themselves, aside from paying lip service to general science education and proposing some utopian schemes for its implementation, most seem resigned (content?) to receive public support that is not based on the public's direct access to what transpires in laboratories nor, for that matter, on any understanding of how science in the laboratory eventuates in the benefits claimed on its behalf.

In this respect, our Martians concede, science reproduces key features of the modern nation-state that still, largely, underwrites scientific research: the stability of both rests on the public's willingness to exchange direct participation in the political process for the promise of expert administration to their basic needs, or 'welfare'. Science extends its constituency of believers by extending its technological benefits, which are said to possess all the distinctive features of scientific knowledge – objectivity, reliability, utility, etc. – *except* a susceptibility to public intervention. All told, then, it would seem that because the average difference in the knowledge of the experts and the public in the case of science is much greater than in that of any organized religion, Earthly faith in science marks a degree of deference to authority that is unprecedented in human history. This unprecedented level of deference is rationalized by an analogy that humans implicitly draw between the inevitability of the physical division of labour and a supposedly corresponding mental division of labour. Thus, just as it is impossible for people to do everything for themselves in the manner of Robinson Crusoe, it is (allegedly) impossible for people to *think* for themselves in all cases. Under the circumstances, a sense of mutual 'trust' is elevated from a necessary evil to a positive virtue in a complex world.[5]

At this point, our Martians anticipate that a human overhearing these ruminations may object that, in the case of religion, the public is usually indoctrinated into convenient falsehoods, or myths. For example, Christians are taught to take Biblical stories, if not as literal truths, then at least as directly applicable to their lives in ways that would probably cause discomfort to the average theologian. However, our Martian friends observe that the situation seems to be just a bit *worse* with regard to science. After all, not only the public, but also practising scientists themselves believe in the myth of *progress*, whereby every scientific achievement is treated as an advance towards the 'Truth'. Indeed, scientists are typically more hostile than the lay public to the demystifying approach to science associated with an anthropology of science. This suggests that scientists may believe that progress is more than a myth, after all. An irreverent but not inappropriate analogy is the difference between telling children that Santa Claus does not exist and telling that to someone who thinks he is Santa. The latter case is tougher to make, so it may be a while before scientists realize that their metaphorical beards and paunches are false.

By now, the Martians are showing signs of cross-cultural strain. Thus, they entertain a third and more radical option: instead of doing anthropology, why not do *archaeology*? Why not wait until humans annihilate each other – an inevitability, they reckon – and then sort through their curious scientific rituals in peace and quiet. (The advent of neutron bomb technology on Earth facilitates this possibility.) Given that humans believe that scientific knowledge not only transcends their devotional rituals but also underwrites the lasting achievements of their most advanced societies, it should be possible for Martians with an adequate command of the major Earthly tongues to reconstruct an ideal version of human civiliz-ation by applying the best scientific theories in the appropriate set-tings.[6] One interesting Earthly objection to this strategy has been presented in the context of 'uninventing' nuclear weapons, with engineers failing to transmit to the next generation the hands-on experience needed to build them.[7] Thus, the atomic equipment pur-chases made by some tyrant will be for naught if no engineers are available with experience in turning plutonium into bombs; a wishful thought, to be sure, one born of a robust belief in the sanc-tity of what the philosophical chemist Michael Polanyi (1891–1976) originally called *tacit knowledge*.[8] This scenario proposes that because the exact knowledge needed for assembling a nuclear bomb is not normally codified, it can be easily lost if not actively maintained.

However, the history of technology on Earth demonstrates many cases of 'reinventing the wheel', by which one culture without prior contact with another culture constructs functionally equivalent devices, once having reached a comparable level of material and technical advancement. Given such cases, it would seem that if one were serious about uninventing nuclear weapons, one would need to do more than eliminate the tacit dimension of building bombs. One would also have to eliminate much of what is written in today's physics and engineering textbooks, upon which bomb manufacture builds. What all this shows is that constructing nuclear bombs is really no different from constructing, say, automobiles. Originally, automotive knowledge also seemed 'tacit' because there were not enough functioning vehicles to determine how many different ways an automobile could be built. However, after an intense trial-and-error period of about twenty years at the start of the twentieth century, many of the possibilities had been explored, and Henry Ford (1863–1947) had even discovered how to mass produce cars on an assembly line. Because international treaties ban the testing of nuclear weapons, humans have failed to see a similar routinization of their manufacture, so it has been easy to conclude that the building of nuclear bombs requires special skills that can easily be lost.[9]

So is archaeology the way to go, after all? Unfortunately, this tempting idea runs foul of the simple fact that, with no humans around, the Martians can never tell whether they have selected the right codified theories and applied them in the right ways. There is no guarantee that the best documented fields of scientific knowledge will turn out to be the most important for understanding science's pivotal place in human civilization. Much of scientific knowledge may have become integrated into ordinary personal habits and social relations. In other words, contrary to the myth of tacit knowledge, it is not that this knowledge could not be codified in principle; rather, as a matter of fact humans would have deemed it too obvious to mention on a regular basis.

Only one anthropological strategy remains. The Martians will have to go to Earth and confront the humans with their own science-based standards of rationality. Humans are certainly used to being held accountable to standards they avow. Indeed, such accountability is itself an extension of the scientific method, as it judges what people say against what they do; in this case, what they say about the nature of science against the data of their behaviour in scientifi-cally relevant settings. Moreover, the genre of human literature known as 'science fiction' is populated with beings whose alien character comes from applying, not strictly alien standards, but rather humanly recognizable standards with a consistency rarely found among the humans themselves. (Imagine the personification of science's superego, say, Mr Spock from *Star Trek.*) Among the advantages of this 'Spockian' approach to Martian anthropology is that it avoids the main objection to science's ability to judge the rationality of native cultures. The Martians note that one of Earth's leading twentieth-century philosophers, Ludwig Wittgenstein, first speculated about the incomparability, or 'incommensurability', of cultural standards after reading James George Frazer's *The Golden Bough: a Study in Comparative Religion* (1890–1915).[10] Wittgenstein diagnosed the wholesale irrationality that Frazer observed in native magical practices in terms of Frazer's own failure to see that his scientific standard of rationality was not theirs. Indeed, the magnitude of the irrationality that Frazer detected across cultures can be traced to the parochialism of his own conception of rationality, one that failed to appreciate any conception of the causal order other than the billiard-ball universe implied by Newtonian mechanics. However, Wittgenstein's objections would not apply in the case under discussion, since *we* are the natives who claim to be scientific.

Moreover, by accepting our standards of scientific rationality at face value, the Martians realize that they cannot argue that our society exhibits a deep, 'adaptive' sense of rationality that transcends people's avowed standards of rationality and hence explains what on the surface may appear to be irrational behaviour. In anticipation of what follows, the Martians observe that Earthly sociobiologists or neoclassical economists often seem to want to save the word 'rationality' by weakening its meaning beyond all recognition. Thus, 'rationality' becomes synonymous with whatever happens to eventuate in a community's long-term survival, regardless of what the people who constitute the community think they are doing or feel about it. However, our Martians refuse to succumb to this semantic legerdemain. In fact, they are inclined to reverse the causal arrows here: that is, to explain the persistence of subverted rationality in terms of *sublimation* rather than transcendence. Thus, our Martian friends rely heavily on what social psychologists call *adaptive preference formations*: mental mechanisms that enable humans to tolerate and rationalize the suboptimal states that result from their failure to abide consistently by the norms of scientific rationality (which includes, of course, their failure to realize that they have so failed).[11]

So, armed with their new anthropological strategy, the Martians begin in a way perversely reminiscent of Frazer: is humanity's faith in science superstitious? The anthropologist Bronislaw Malinowski (1884–1942) used 'superstition' as a technical term for the tendency of natives to assume a necessary causal connection between two events that occur in close spatial or temporal proximity to each other.[12] Consider the case of natives who believe that their dancing leads to rain. Anthropologists were quick to observe that even in these extreme cases, the natives timed their dancing so that it correlated with more direct indicators of the onset of rain. In other words, the success of the rain dance was usually determined by these other events. While the rain dance was clearly superstitious when taken on its own terms, its persistence as an institution could be explained by its relationship to other causally relevant factors, not least ones contributing to a sense of solidarity among the natives themselves.

The Martians now propose to turn this sort of analysis on science. The first step is to take stock of the two most general philosophical orientations to knowledge, *relativism* and *realism*.[13] Curiously, these complementary world-views seem to be founded on dubious, if not strictly fallacious, reasoning. Their pedigrees can be traced to the history of religion. In this context, relativism meant that God is already within each creature, whereas realism implied that God is the goal towards which all creatures strive. In science, the relativist argues that the beliefs and actions of native cultures serve functions comparable to ones in a scientific culture, so the natives must be rational because scientific culture certainly cannot be irrational. The Martians note that this is an interesting strategy for insulating one's own culture from critical scrutiny, which works by refusing to spot errors in other cultures lest similar errors be spotted in one's own. Earthly philosophers call this strategy the *principle of charity*. In contrast, the realist argues that the familiar story of scientific progress would be a miracle if scientists were not in the process of getting closer to the nature of reality. Of course, the Martians observe, the realist fails to observe that a story with such odds one way or the other is probably just false, or at least not properly told. The strategy here seems to be to impoverish the imagination of alternative accounts of the history of science so that one has no choice but to believe in the truth of the one remaining account. Philosophers dignify this strategy with the name *transcendental argument*.

   In their attempts to navigate between the Scylla of charity and
the Charybdis of transcendence, our Martians think that a more
direct approach would be to enumerate the ways in which contemporary science policy reproduces five traditional categories of
religious thought: *mystery, soteriology, saintliness, magic causation*,
and *theodicy.* These categories have been subject to extensive cross-
cultural study as instances of rationality slipping into rationalization.[14] In each case an element of superstition is involved which
obscures the causal mechanisms relevant for understanding a range
of social phenomena.

Mystery

This is the paradox of science being both everywhere and nowhere
at the same time. Humans have a hard time deciding whether science is only an elite and perhaps declining feature of their society
or the ether in which all of human society transpires. On the one
hand, most public and private institutions do not spend more than
2–3 per cent on research and development, and since the end of the
Cold War science enrolments have generally dropped. On the other
hand, if one counts all the jobs that require some level of scientific
or technical training, then it would seem that 40 per cent of the
workforce is, as they say, 'knowledge-intensive'.[15] Some pundits
have gone so far as to claim that scientific knowledge is the primary
factor of production in today's economy. But on closer inspection,
'science' here seems to operate as a 'god of the gaps': specifically,
whatever it takes to explain why the same amount of labour and
capital now enables more work to be done than ever before.[16] For
example, if Japan outproduces Britain, it is thought to be because
the Japanese 'know' something that the British do not. However,
there is little agreement on what it is that the Japanese know, how
they know it, or whether the British would appreciably improve
their economic position by mastering this knowledge. Armed with
such a subtle yet pervasive conception of scientific knowledge,
humans are then able to focus on differences in qualities of mind
and ignore explanations that appeal to more mundane features of
social, political, and economic relations. The narrowness of this
conception is often masked as humans nowadays tend to fall back
on the politically correct word 'culture' to characterize supposedly
salient differences between, say, the British and Japanese 'minds'.

Yet the mystery of scientific knowledge runs still deeper, in a way that may be summed up as *the military–industrial metaphor*. This metaphor fuses two countervailing ways of talking about knowledge that humans employ interchangeably and without much distress. The military side of the metaphor represents knowledge as inquiry, which is to say, a goal-oriented activity whose target is the 'Truth' about one's domain of inquiry. Inquirers approximate this target to varying degrees. Since the target is typically taken to be hidden from view – 'behind the appearances' – no one ever scores a direct hit. Yet, since the times of the ancient Athenians, inquirers have been judged by the artfulness of their strategies and tactics. Education, from this angle, is target practice of a rather abstract sort that calls to mind the spirit of gamesmanship in which, to this day, humans often take examinations. In its military guise, knowledge is leisured, sporting, and crafty, revealing as much incisiveness with as little effort as possible. An 'elegant' mathematical proof is, perhaps, the paradigm case of this conception of scientific knowledge.

By contrast, the industrial side of the metaphor refers to knowledge as a laborious process that displays much handiwork and issues in products of various sorts, usually with the understanding that more of them is always better than fewer. Indeed, from the industrial angle, knowledge is indefinitely accumulated. Here education becomes a form of craft apprenticeship, whereby one acquires the tools and skills needed to produce more knowledge products, not to mention more knowledge producers. The opposing pulls of the military and industrial sides of the metaphor can be numerically represented in terms of the distinction between *intensive* and *extensive* magnitudes: that is, the difference between approximating an end to varying degrees and increasing a dimension without an end in sight.

The denizens of the original Western universities – the thirteenth-century scholastics lecturing at Paris and Oxford – first experienced the tension inherent in the military–industrial metaphor as they sought to recover an essentially aristocratic rhetoric of inquiry (epitomized in the Socratic dialogues) to legitimate what had become a highly technical form of manual labour, specifically one based on writing. Needless to say, this tension has only become more pronounced since that time, as the development of both sides of the metaphor has stretched it to bursting point. On the military side, the goals of inquiry and society have been fused together in a generalized doctrine of *progress* whereby the ultimate scientific theory would deliver the means for governing the ideal society. On the industrial side, great science has been increasingly identified with *Big Science*, as if success at securing funds for an expensive research project were itself an indirect indicator of the project's potential contribution to scientific knowledge. When appealing for public support, scientists like to conflate the two images, typically by presenting a torrent of publications as evidence for their closing in on the fundamental principles of the bit of reality to which they lay claim.

However, the global consequences of these attempts at playing off the latent contradictions of the military–industrial metaphor are self-defeating. While there is evidence that the nations with the lion's share of research funding generate an even larger share of the total number of scientific publications, there is also evidence that each additional increment in research investment advances the frontiers of knowledge a little less than the previous one. In other words, *accelerating* the rate at which scientific publications are produced is perfectly compatible with *decelerating* the rate at which agreement is reached on the solutions to a field's fundamental problems.[17] The overall image of the dynamics of scientific inquiry, then, is one of a goal that seems to recede the more vigorously it is pursued. Tantalus would have appreciated the ruse![18]

Soteriology

These are the stories that make science the key to human salvation by presenting the peculiar history surrounding the rise of Western science as a blueprint of stages through which all aspiring cultures must pass. Interestingly, this idea has had enormous cross-ideological appeal. Entrepreneurial capitalists claim that science inspires the innovations needed to expand and restructure the market, whereas Marxist socialists believe that science-based technologies will level class divisions between labour and management, and enable an adequate provision of goods and services for everyone. Nevertheless, both sides agree that science is the only feature of human culture that has made irreversible progress.[19] However, contrary to these sentiments, non-Western cultures that remained uncolonized by the West have eclectically mixed scientific and native practices in ways that confound the image of a universal blueprint for scientific progress. Japan's meteoric rise to global prominence after centuries of isolation proves to be the object lesson, which in turn caused Western historians to rethink the exact source of science's power. (We shall explore the implications of this point in Chapter 6.)

The fact that polar ideologies can take comfort in the history of science suggests that there is more to the history than meets the eye. Take the natural sciences' moment of epiphany, the 'Scientific Revolution' that allegedly occurred in northwestern Europe in the seventeenth century. Given its purported trans-historical significance, it is rather striking that it went unnamed until the 1940s (when it appeared in the writings of Herbert Butterfield and Alexandre Koyré), and that, even to this day, its exact time of occurrence remains contested, since two centuries passed before the experimental practices of Galileo, Boyle, and Newton were made a regular part of university education.[20] This suggests that the scientifically devout are resorting to the time-honoured literary device of *syncretism*, whereby historical events significantly separated in time and space are collapsed into one continuous episode – an extended present – in order to heighten their collective momentousness. The extended present is often captured in the image of the past as the womb bearing the seeds of the present. This is the doctrine of *hysteresis*, which is exemplified by the influential view of science as driven by paradigms, put forth by Kuhn. Each paradigm is named after its founder, such as Newton, Darwin, or Einstein, and scientists' sense of self seems to be guided by the image of their standing on the shoulders of one or more of these giants, to paraphrase Newton.

For example, according to one influential view, the 'rationality' of science lies in the personal biases of scientists miraculously can celling each other out through long term interaction. As Popper famously put it, each scientist is his own conjecturer and his neighbour's refuter. However, the 'long term' turns out to put a perverse spin on Popper's dictum, as increased investment in unrefuted science makes any subsequent refutation more expensive to lodge. Thus, 'progress' in science can be most easily discerned in a field such as high-energy physics, in which so much has already been invested in a specific research trajectory that it is no longer feasible to question the wisdom of its continued pursuit. Our Martian friends are struck by the strangeness of a supposedly 'universal' form of knowledge whose pursuit is increasingly restricted to the wealthier peoples of the world. But even in these wealthy nations, science students have found – in the absence of war or some other national emergency – that their suitability for employment is no greater than that of their humanistic colleagues. In both cases, about 35 per cent find work related to their academic training.[21] However, whereas one frequently hears complaints about an over-production of humanists, the surplus of scientists making their way into non-scientific jobs is applauded as a testimony to the 'versatility' of scientific training and the rationalization of society that is heralded by this diffusion of scientific talent.

'Cross-disciplinary fertilization' turns out to be a hopeful way of talking about the fact that universities always lag behind changing job markets by producing many scientists who need to find work in fields other than the ones in which they were trained. Admittedly, sometimes this has led to the establishment of new disciplines, as in the case of the ambitious young German physiologist, Wilhelm Wundt (1832–1920), who migrated to philosophy to found the science of experimental psychology by adapting medical instruments to test hypotheses about the relationship between mind and body.[22] However, the Martian anthropologist wonders whether this science would have emerged without the labour market problem and, more pointedly, whether much would have been lost without its emergence. Indeed, it would be interesting to record the reaction of scientists who are confronted with these accounts of the unintended benefits that their otherwise undesirable actions bestow on their colleagues.

Saintliness

Because success in science is always elusive, scientists dedicate themselves unconditionally to their vocation. Such devotion even figures in how economists rationalize the fact that the salaries of distinguished academic scientists are, on average, not much higher than those of undistinguished ones.[23] They presume that devotion is its own reward, with the distinguished scientists manifesting more of it, in lieu of income. But under the Martian gaze, this economy of the spirit appears itself to be elusive. Might not a simpler explanation for the small salary spread be that the 'less distinguished' scientists excel in teaching and/or administration, whereas the 'distinguished' ones are devoted exclusively to research? One's own sense of sacrifice may strike another as a principled refusal to violate one's sense of self-interest. At the very least, it suggests that 'scientist' is, strictly speaking, less a category of employment and more a state of mind about how one's employment is regarded.

One species of the sacrificial scientist, the *genius*, typically confounds all expectations by making an extraordinary discovery while working under adverse intellectual and financial circumstances. Indeed, humans appear hard-pressed to identify any genius who did not suffer hardship, be it prior neglect or scanty material resources, although that biographical fact is officially irrelevant to what makes someone a genius. Nevertheless, tales of the fame and rewards ultimately bestowed on such people motivate scientists who would otherwise be deterred by their low probability of success. Economists have even tried to formalize the extent of this success by deeming scientific knowledge a 'public' or 'ethereal' good, which means that the only real effort is expended by the person(s) who make a scientific finding, whereas the originator's successors can, in principle, use that finding without having to expend comparable effort. The Martians immediately observe that this analysis conveniently leaves out the expense incurred by consumers in acquiring the background knowledge needed to make use of the genius's discovery.[24] By luring people in this fashion, science ensures a more competitive pool of talent, as the rate of scientific success does not appreciably increase by more people participating in it; if anything, it drops.[25]

If the best scientists willingly sacrifice themselves, the rest are helped on to the sacrificial pyre by government funding policies that are functionally equivalent to the triaging of medical services. The scientists favoured are the ones most likely to accomplish big things in the shortest time. The tendency of taking from the strong to compensate the weak that is characteristic of distributive justice appears to have no place in science policy. Scientists' training, first appointments, and publications are remarkably good indicators of their prospects as published researchers. Consequently, many policy makers have gone so far as to argue that 'the man' [*sic*] rather than the project should be the basis for science funding decisions.

Unfortunately, this policy fails to distinguish between *rewarding* and *reinforcing* scientific endeavour. Precious resources are tied up in scientists persisting in the same pious rituals that first brought them success. Instead, our Martians think, it should be possible to reward scientists for past achievement without encouraging them to pursue the same line of research in perpetuity. What all this shows is that, regarded as a system of personal ethics, science does an excellent job of reminding its practitioners (and the public) what it is like to be *perfect* but offers little guidance on how to *improve*. (These career-related issues will be considered in more depth in Appendix 2 to this report.)

This section concludes with some remarks 'for discussion only' on the proposition that the 'uneven development' between the advance of cutting-edge research and its assimilation by the rest of the human population could be ameliorated by removing science's last social prejudice, namely, its tendency to set admission requirements that favour those who appear most intelligent on the basis of standardized aptitude tests and various measures of academic performance. Science would better earn its reputation for producing a 'universal' form of knowledge, our Martians hypothesize, if into its ranks were incorporated a wider spectrum of Earthly intelligence. After all, if part of the point of doing science – especially in its experimental mode – is to check taken-for-granted preconceptions, then this principle should be applied across the board, including science itself, especially its tendency for those 'in the know' to dismiss a speculation out of hand because it conflicts with what the experts currently take for granted about the domain of reality that they administer. Indeed, one way of interpreting the 'saintliness' of geniuses like Newton and Darwin who laboured hard against perceived resistance to their ideas is that they could not quite grasp why the 'obvious objections' should be taken as decisive, and hence they persisted in lines of inquiry that a more 'clever' scientist would have avoided at the outset because they could 'instantly see' that it would amount to naught. Admittedly, both Newton and Darwin were never explicitly told that they were too dull to make revolutionary breakthroughs in science; but then the current educational selection mechanisms for who becomes a scientist were not yet in place. Of course, since humans started to preselect people for scientific careers, there have been no geniuses of the calibre of Newton and Darwin (if any): spurious correlation – or not?

Magic Causation

'Action at a distance' is behind the idea that the sheer addition of
scientists or their (highly cited) publications will automatically
increase overall human technical capability or, better still, human
welfare. The magic works by examining the 'impact' of scientific
research over such an expanded time frame that the most arcane
physical theory can be shown to have issued in the most mundane
practical products; hence, Newtonian mechanics is alleged to have
'caused' the Industrial Revolution a hundred years later. But rather
than see this as an argument for making the link between theory
and practice tighter, it is read as more reason for continuing to keep
them apart, as the mere intent to be practical is thought to vitiate
the spirit of honest inquiry. Strangely, the humans never ask the
counterfactual question of whether the Industrial Revolution might
have occurred even without Newton's great discoveries.[26] Correspondingly, they do not ask whether the call for additional research
may be a way to delay the implementation of certain policies of
social change, as when tobacco and chemical companies devote
enormous sums to conduct ever more thorough scientific studies on
the toxicity of their products. In short, the motto of the scrupulous
scientific methodologist – 'Correlation is not causation' – can be
taken in a Machiavellian manner as a recipe for political procrasti-
nation.

Our Martians are intrigued by the extent to which humans will
focus on the funding of innovative, even 'blue sky', research, while
simply take for granted that these innovations will somehow
become readily available to society at large. This tendency also
operates retrospectively. Consider the case of Alfred Nobel
(1833–96), the Swedish inventor of dynamite who, in his will,
endowed what have become the most prestigious annual awards for
scientific achievement. Nobel specifically stipulated that the prizes
bearing his name should be given to those whose works have most
benefited humanity, yet the prize committees consist of disciplinary
specialists who mainly reward research that has had major impact
on themselves and their colleagues. But even historians, especially
when they cover wide spatiotemporal expanses, tend to presume
that once a scientific discovery has overcome its original academic
critics, it thereby becomes a publicly accessible domain of knowledge. All of this invites expectations about the instantaneous

reception of contemporary scientific developments, which, when they fail to materialize, lead policy makers to proclaim that their societies have entered a decadent, anti-scientific phase. It would seem that this particular form of alarmism could be arrested by ensuring that general histories of science cover not only successive research frontiers but also the long struggles surrounding science education, publication, and application. These are less glamorous topics perhaps, but ones more relevant to a rational science policy.

Magic causation is brought out very nicely in two sorts of questions that scientists often pose when the unconditional authority of their knowledge is challenged:

1 Why do humans trust aeroplanes to deliver them unharmed to their destinations?
2 Why do humans recoil from the prospect of walking out of windows in skyscrapers?

Sincere answers to both questions are supposed to reveal the extent to which people take for granted the validity of science in their everyday activities.

In the case of 1, to the extent that the average human has any knowledge of what keeps an aeroplane in flight, that knowledge probably relies on basic principles of aerodynamics, most of which were known by the early nineteenth century, if not earlier. However, this immediately raises the question of whether the people holding these beliefs can explain why it then took another century before reliably airborne craft were in general circulation. As it turns out, people have little or no knowledge of the feats of engineering required, which, in many cases, have been achieved without any deep knowledge of the relevant physical principles. The Wright brothers, who finally succeeded in producing the first heavier-than-air craft in 1903, worked in a bicycle shop in Dayton, Ohio.[27] Even today, an aeroplane flies because of a coordinated network of operations that involve the skill of engineers, pilots, ground support staff, and many others, with physicists found only at the periphery of these activities. The failure of any of these people to behave as expected can subvert the aeroplane's flight. In practice, then, the regular use of aeroplanes as a mode of transport is implicitly (that is, from the Martian standpoint) a ratification of a belief in the stability of these social relationships. Knowledge of aerodynamics may work, at a pinch, to explain the workings of an aircraft, if one lacks any specific knowledge of its production team or flight record, but to reduce the airborne capabilities of such a craft to the 'application of science' is as much wishful thinking and hand-waving as claiming that an 'infusion of the Holy Spirit' is responsible for its airworthiness. At most, both explain why certain possibilities are ruled out by nature but not why the actual case is ruled in. Thus, our Martians conclude, the fact that humans appeal to science to justify their beliefs is not sufficient to render those beliefs rational.

In the case of 2, it is true that humans refer to a force called 'gravity' to explain why they do not routinely walk out of windows. However, the idea that things heavier than air tend to fall to the ground is one that humans picked up early in their collective existence, probably as a prerequisite of their continued survival. Modern physical science is, historically speaking, a johnny-come-lately to this primordial insight. The novelty, if not eccentricity, provided by physics lies exclusively in the explanation it offers for the insight. Indeed, when people are asked to explain what they mean by 'gravity', they are likely to speak in a way that is more reminiscent of Aristotle than Newton, let alone Einstein. In other words, they conceive of gravity as very much an Earthbound force, and not a universal principle of physical attraction. The implicit difference between scientists and non-scientists on this point can be readily understood in terms of the two groups using rather different categorical schemes to classify phenomena. Whereas the physicist wants an account of physical force that can encompass all moving bodies, both on Earth and in the heavens, the aspirations of the average human are much more modest, and hence much less abstract. Even when non-scientists have been schooled in the scientific ways of explaining their experiences of falling bodies, they revert to their old ways once out of the classroom, since they fit more intuitively into the world they inhabit on a daily basis.[28]

Although scientists routinely deplore this intellectual recidivism, they may do better to take a page from the history of social science and acknowledge that the stability of social life persists even after a belief in social 'laws' and 'forces' has disappeared, and that maybe the quoted expressions reflect more a value preference on the part of scientists than a brute fact about what scientists study.[29] Here we see very clearly the extent to which magic causation reflects a kind of *methodological ventriloquism*, whereby scientists frequently project their descriptive and explanatory categories upon an indifferent reality and an unobliging public.

Theodicy

This is literally the attempt to fathom God's sense of justice. Applied to the case at hand, it is the widespread human belief that even the most loathsome features of science, if they persist long enough, must have some redeeming value. From the earliest days of Christianity, there have been speculations about how each creature and event functioned in the divine plan. Indeed, starting with St Augustine (AD354–430), events that appeared to do much harm and little good were taken to be signs that the ends of Creation were ultimately beyond human comprehension. The more intellectually ambitious natural theologians then turned to theodicy to study how apparent liabilities – such as monstrous births, natural disasters, and human atrocities – may be seen as contributing to an overall picture of ours being 'the best of all possible worlds', the only kind of world that an omnipotent and omnibenevolent God could create. By the late seventeenth century, as much of this theorizing began to lose its theological baggage, philosophers like Gottfried von Leibnitz (1646–1716) spoke of the *economy of nature,* governed by the *principle of sufficient reason.* This principle enjoined the inquirer to seek the end that would be served by a given event, if we presume that the event is part of the most efficient means to that end. In short, one was to rationalize the event as a 'means' rather than to question it as an 'end'.

To be sure, the Leibnitzian inquirer was satirized as Dr Pangloss in Voltaire's *Candide* (1759). Pangloss simply assumed that there is a point to everything that happens and that any alternative action would have been worse. This sentiment would continue into the nineteenth and twentieth centuries in the guise of 'functionalist' and 'evolutionary' thinking. Supposedly, there is something charmed about the mere existence of stable social or biological systems, even when these systems maintain their 'equilibrium' at the cost of the oppression, waste, and death to some of their parts. Whoever's ends may be served by this process, they are most certainly *not* those who must bear the burden of these 'costs'. But then, whose ends are served? 'Spirit' and 'life' acquire rhetorical force here, as they seem eligible to subsist through a succession of expendable and replaceable material parts. More mechanistic thinkers, ranging from Herbert Spencer (1820–1903) to Herbert Simon (b. 1916), have put the point less metaphysically, claiming that evolution is the story of how organisms come up with increasingly more sophisticated means to achieve the same old ends. But here, too, 'ends' remains radically underdefined, typically glossed by an empirically self-fulfilling term such as 'survival'.

Nowhere is this last point more evident than in contemporary philosophical accountings for science, especially the so-called *invisible hand* account.[30] The basic strategy here is to account for scientific progress in terms of the spontaneous self-interested transactions of scientists, which over time have been conventionalized as *peer review*. Implicit in this view is a relatively abundant and unregulated material environment for science. Peer review works not only because scientists have an interest in criticizing each other, but also because the scientific community is sufficiently endowed to enable scientists to receive exactly the resources that their peers deem their research to merit. The Martian observers then ask, has science reached an optimal level of deregulation? Would an even *more* invisible hand produce still better science?

Given the rarity with which humans pose these questions, it would seem that appeals to the invisible hand are indeed tantamount to a rationalization of the status quo. By contrast, a principled libertarian like Paul Feyerabend (1924–94) wanted to push invisibility to the limit.[31] He anticipated that the next step in the deregulation of scientific inquiry would be the decentralization of the science funding apparatus, preferably by curtailing the state's ability to concentrate wealth through taxation. Only a policy environment that is insulated from democratic processes, Feyerabend reasoned, would tolerate a research programme whose survival depends on monopolizing the material resources available for inquiry. For example, no one ever put the scientific 'megaprojects' of our time – including the Superconducting Supercollider and the Human Genome Project – to a formal vote of either the populace or, for that matter, the scientific community. The US Congress funded both projects with taxpayers' money, simply on the basis of elite, and often self-serving, scientific testimony.

The Martians then offer some historical perspective on this point. One may believe that the Charter of the Royal Society of London in 1660 marked the beginning of a spontaneously self-organizing system of inquirers, yet the intellectual descendents of the Royal Society's founders may have become victims of the advantages that the natural sciences have accumulated over the past 350 years. Specifically, as the sciences have participated in the material reproduction of society, scientists have lost not only the flexibility to change their own research trajectories on the basis of peer criticism, but also a sense of tolerance for many competing trajectories. Too much else is at stake for scientists to judge knowledge claims on their merits alone. Hence, Feyerabend's policy advice: today's scientists should not inherit the accumulated advantage of their precursors, even if that means divesting support for research projects currently touted by the elite members of the scientific community.

Conclusion and recommendations

Appealing to scientific authority has proved to be the most palatable means for democratic governments to coerce the people of Earth. However, these governments are now saddled with enormous budgetary deficits, mostly arising from the need to buffer the effects that rapidly changing economic conditions have on their constituency. Under these circumstances, it is easy to see why the USA finally abandoned plans to construct the world's largest particle accelerator, the Superconducting Supercollider, despite its promise to uncover the ultimate building blocks of matter. The Martian anthropologists then wonder, what if this is only the beginning of a trend towards governments divesting their financial interest in the education and research of the scientific community?

They conclude that this would be equivalent to *secularizing* science, in the sense that Christendom was secularized when the emerging nation-states of Europe in the seventeenth century refused to grant a single Church special economic and political privileges. This led to a period of evangelism, in which religious believers competed to attract believers who would materially sustain their efforts.[32] Analogues of such proselytizing efforts can already be seen among the defenders of New Age knowledges who broadcast their 'infomercials' on late-night cable television. They promise custom-made enlightenment at a price (of a video, a book, or a therapy session). In the next few decades, we may find IBM or Shell Oil publicizing their virtues in terms of the major projects in high-energy physics or molecular biology they have supported, which may be used to excuse whatever political or ecological indiscretions were involved in their support. It will be interesting to see the role that will be played by all those disappointed natural science degree holders who were misled into thinking that there was a market for pure inquiry.

Opponents to the secularization model argue that science's demonstrated ability to transform the material world far outstrips that of organized religion, and that this difference warrants the exalted status that science continues to enjoy. This argument seems intuitively persuasive to humans because they tend to mismatch the features of 'science' and 'religion' under comparison. Taken in isolation, the laboratory touted as the original site of a scientific discovery has no more transformative capacity than a cathedral where High Mass is regularly held. The laboratory becomes an Archimedean lever capable of moving the world only once we add other laboratories, as well as the political and economic clout needed to convert the laboratory's eccentric events into well founded, mass-produced technical knowledge.[33] Indeed, the denizens of Christendom are best compared with those putative inhabitants of an 'information society', as suggested earlier in the discussion of science's 'mysterious' character.

A proper comparison between religion and science would have to start with a world religion: one with a network of spiritual and material resources comparable to those of science. One must then take care not to beg the question by supposing that the technological feats of, say, Christian and Muslim cultures resulted from their having 'implicitly mastered' scientific principles, especially ones that would become fully known only after the Scientific Revolution. That way of putting matters makes no more (and no less) sense than claiming that contemporary scientific achievements in physics and chemistry are moments in the revelation of God's Word. Indeed, the heroes of the Scientific Revolution were themselves inclined to explain their virtuosity in science by their virtuosity in religion, and not the other way around. Moreover, such explanations continue to thrive in the avowedly pro-scientific environment of Islamic fundamentalism. At a deeper level, the very idea of comparing the efficacy of religion and science may seem perverse, since many of the same people, institutions, and bodies of knowledge have been involved in the two activities. The difference between the practice of something called 'religion' and something called 'science' would seem to lie in the reasons given for pursuing the practice as well as the conditions under which it is pursued. With respect to these issues, our understanding of religion is much better than our understanding of science. The secularization model enables the Martians to use the history of religion to make sense of the future of science. On that basis, they envisage humans embarking on a second Enlightenment, one in which science continues to enjoy popular support even after, like Christendom, its sacred status and state support have been removed.

It would be interesting, in future research, to pursue a comparison of the 'disunity' of scientific disciplines and the emergence of multi-denominational Christianity. It has been argued that when Europe was united as 'Christendom', contradictory elements of Church doctrine – such as the idea that the One True God consists of 'three persons' – were neutralized in practices that stressed different elements on different occasions. However, with secularization came the elimination of many of these buffering practices, which in turn served to make the doctrinal contradictions appear stark and irresolvable.[34] Similarly, if the end of state funding for science were to end the perception of a unified conception of science, the fact that the physical, life, and social sciences operate with fundamentally different aims and orientations would perhaps rise to the surface to become a point of public contention. In any case, the public already seems to have an instinctively clearer sense of such cross-disciplinary differences than practising scientists who, despite their clear theoretical and methodological differences, continue to talk in terms of a 'Science' common to them all. Indeed, what scientists often see as the public's 'confusion' about the nature of science may simply be the public's recognition that there is no 'nature' to science.

Appendices

The *Martian Ultraviolet Paper* contains two appendices. The first consists of an examination of the four organizational norms of science proposed by Robert Merton (b. 1910).[35] The Martians describe Merton as a 'sociological scholastic' for having derived the norms, not from any first-hand observation of science in action, but from the authoritative testimony of the most esteemed scientists and their philosophical well-wishers. (Imagine a sociologist deriving the norms of religion by looking exclusively at the pronouncements of priests and prophets.) The second appendix concerns an analysis of the peculiar history of the *Science Citation Index*, which our Martian friends portray as a relatively primitive information search technology that has managed to become a standard of scientific performance and a symbol of the so-called *Knowledge Society* that Earthbound intellectuals generally seem to think they inhabit.

Appendix 1: The Mertonian norms

The Martians begin by reminding the reader that, as their discussion of theodicy has shown, humans suffer from profound value confusion on matters relating to science. Basically, we stand accused of excusing any stable pattern of scientific behaviour by manipulating the frame of reference within which its effects are regarded. The Martians thus propose to show that Merton's famous norms can be read in a diabolical light simply by shifting the frame of reference from the scientific community as such to the larger society in which that community is embedded.[36] They want to show that the norms may indeed pick out real aspects of science, but that these aspects could be just as easily presented in ways that would strongly discourage a society from fostering the pursuit of science. Whereas Earthbound sociologists have stressed the failure of Merton's norms to exert any determinate force on research practice, because they can be used to justify opposing courses of action, the Martians argue that the relevant indeterminacy pertains not to the force of the norms as such but to whether that force is interpreted as good or bad.[37] They then suggest that further research into this matter must examine the mechanics of the educational system, so as to explain how both professional scientists and the lay public acquire a positive rather than a negative 'spin' on the norms. The Martians encapsulate their results in Figure 4.1. The *normative underdetermination of science* refers to the fact that the same scientific norms can be given alternatively valued spins, according to the context in which they are regarded. An explanation of this point for each of the four norms follows.

According to the norm of *universalism*, science is not culturally specific but contains truths both by and for all people (as opposed to claims that have been made on behalf of, say, 'Aryan science').

Merton's positive spin	Martian negative spin
Universalism	Cultural imperalism
Communism	Mafiosism
Disinterestedness	Opportunism
Organized scepticism	Collective irresponsibility

Figure 4.1   The normative underdetermination of science.

Aside from Merton's own appeals to the pronouncements of interested parties (namely, leading scientists and philosophers of
science), what might be cited to support the presence of this norm?
Natural scientists from all over the world must, and do, publish in
the same group of overwhelmingly anglophone journals located in
the USA and the United Kingdom. By contrast, in the social sciences, there is not the same agreement over the most important
journals. Scholars in these fields tend to publish in journals that are
aligned with their specific national and cultural interests. Although
this practice makes the social sciences seem more provincial, it also
escapes the cultural imperialism that passes for universalism in the
natural sciences. If 'imperialism' seems too strong a word, consider
how scientists from the Indian subcontinent endure a cognitive
schizophrenia comparable to that of Indian civil servants during
British imperial rule.[38] Thus, at least some Indian physicists assign
certain culturally specific meanings to terms in the 'universal' language of science that are edited out of their formal communi-
cations. A good example of this process concerns the word 'facility',
officially a term for the place where a major piece of scientific
apparatus is housed, but also a colloquial way of referring to a
toilet. Ethnographic studies of the conversations of Indian physicists reveal that this *double entendre* is quite useful for members of
the elite Brahman caste (from which most physicists come) to
subtly express their disdain for the grubbiness of laboratory work.[39]
No doubt, were this attitude to enter the public record of science,
many Westerners who consider experimentation to be the lifeblood
of science would be up in arms and wonder whether their Indian
colleagues were practising science in 'good faith'. At that point, the
natural sciences would start to acquire the sectarianism that characterizes the social sciences. Luckily (at least for science), self-
censorship is the mark of competence in an imperial regime.

Merton also held that scientists were normative *communists* in that they are committed to sharing data and credit, in contrast to the trade secrets kept by firms that are interested in science only as a means of making money. However, 'sharing' means something a bit more proprietary than Merton's term implies. It is less a matter of assigning collective ownership for an empirical finding than of distributing ownership to others whom the scientist thinks (will think they) deserve it. To speak bluntly, 'communal sharing' amounts to little more than insurance against risk. Although scientists are not, strictly speaking, coerced to share with their colleagues, they are really in no position to choose *not* to do so. Rather, they have an incentive to share because every reason for their not doing so has been removed. If scientists refuse to share, they merely open themselves to negative sanctions. In the future, colleagues have grounds for not sharing with them, approving their grants, or hiring their students. In terms of day-to-day practice, it is nearly impossible to use someone else's apparatus or findings without contacting them for background information not included in the typical scientific article.[40] Thus, one needs to be in the author's good graces. Moreover, because each scientific specialty is dominated by a few gatekeepers who pass judgement on everyone else in the field, failure to appease these 'peers' can be disastrous, much like failure to pay protection money to the local mafia boss. Not surprisingly, scientists tend to underplay their own originality and overplay that of their significant colleagues.

This problem arises less in the social sciences precisely because authority there is so much more fragmented – in virtue of the plethora of journals and interests they represent – that a gatekeeper is less able to prevent an offender from ever publishing again. Nevertheless, whenever field specialists are the exclusive overseers of each other's work, it is susceptible to Mertonian 'communism' for yet another reason. Peers are usually in no position to directly authenticate the work of their colleagues, yet they take collective responsibility for it by publishing it in their official journals or broadcasting it in their professional forums. In that sense, peer review issues authors with intellectual insurance policies in case their results are subject to attack. If the results are shown to be lacking, it will be attributed to honest error and not incompetence or fraud. Thus, while authenticity is judged simply on the basis of the plausibility of the written report, the editors negotiate with

authors the size of the knowledge claim that their articles entitle
them to make, hoping that authors' interest in publication will
cause them to make relatively modest claims.[41]

Scientists' *disinterestedness* lies in the fact that they are not, as a
group, committed to any ideology, and hence (on Merton's telling)
can follow the truth wherever it may lead. However, in practice, disinterestedness is often indistinguishable from opportunism, as most
science is designed to be doable in virtually any cultural setting,
provided there is an appropriate level of material resources and
technical competence. Thus, it is usually possible for scientists to go
to the highest bidder without worrying that their knowledge would
be vitiated in the process. Given sufficient plutonium, former Soviet
physicists can make nuclear bombs that work just as well in Iraq as
in the United States, regardless of their ideological differences.
Indeed, precisely because science itself does not dictate which side
scientists should be on, they are the perfect 'wild cards' in any
balance-of-power struggle. For this reason, as late as the nineteenth
century, the Ottomans and the Chinese regarded the West as bar-
baric in its indiscriminate pursuit of the power that science-based
munitions could bring it. From their standpoint, there was nothing
intellectually profound in a triumph founded on the sheer concentration of force, be it human or technological. Similar reservations
about the wisdom of disinterestedness were expressed within the
Western scientific community in the aftermath of the First World
War, whose unprecedented level of destructiveness was due to the
mass mobilization of scientists, especially chemists. In the wake of
that experience, scientists across a wide range of the ideological
spectrum have tried to constitute the scientific community as its
own interest group, or class, so as to avoid being easily absorbed
into the agendas of the state or industry. Clearly, these efforts failed
to stem the tide of destructiveness during the Second World War,
which is often called the 'physicists' war' because of the key role
played by the founders of nuclear physics in a race between the
Allied and Axis Powers to develop the atomic bomb.

Finally, the *organized scepticism* of scientists lies in their refusal to
take any beliefs for granted until a sound empirical basis has been
found for them, even if these beliefs are cherished by the larger
society. On Merton's reading, this is a mark of intellectual boldness.
But considered in terms of the consequences of putting this norm in
practice, organized scepticism is callous and disorienting. A straight

reading of history would see that the great battles fought in the name of 'science' against various religions and cultural traditions began as backlashes by societies that had already given scientists a measure of tolerance and autonomy, only to find it go unreciprocated, as scientists seemed to want society to grant their views hegemonic status. Thus, Galileo and Darwin spawned major religious reactions only after there had already been a certain measure of tolerance for the sun-centred universe and the evolution of the species, respectively. Were contemporary humans not inclined to see themselves as the long-term beneficiaries of the cultural dislocations caused by the revolutionary scientists of the past, they would probably dismiss 'organized scepticism' as 'collective irresponsibility'. Certainly, scientists do not embrace present-day radicals with the same enthusiasm as they do past ones.

Appendix 2: The Science Citation Index

One of the most peculiar features of the contemporary intellectual scene on Earth is that academic knowledge workers – 'scientists' in the broad sense – have promoted *post-industrialism* just at the time that their own activities have come to approximate the industrial character of advanced capitalism. On the one hand, sociologists starting with Daniel Bell (b. 1919) have been keen to persuade non-academics that history has entered a post-industrial phase. On the other, the expression 'knowledge production' tumbles freely from academic lips and pens.[42] This verbal habit unwittingly exposes the continued captivity of scientists to the old industrial mindset. To sound a familiar Marxist theme, as the meaning of academic labour has come to be identified with its products, the ultimate fates of these products seem increasingly beyond their control. Clearly, this state of affairs applies to the products of research, and specifically books and articles: the more, the faster, the better – and for whose benefit?

Because the capitalization of academia has occurred during a period of unprecedented expansion in the higher education sector, its effects have gone largely uncriticized, if not entirely unnoticed. The twentieth century has witnessed the incorporation of many people into higher education who had traditionally been excluded on the basis of gender, ethnicity, and ideology. Yet the upscaling of the academic enterprise since the Second World War – the increasing numbers of people who have become professional academics along with the enormous resources that have been lavished on university based pursuits – have brought on a more insidious form of marginalization: 'insidious' because it is an *unintended* consequence of the academy's newfound expansiveness. It is the marginalization that results from one's published work going unread, undiscussed, and uncited, and even when cited, cited in an omnibus fashion, as part of a list of names whose company the author had perhaps taken great pains *not* to keep. To put the point in perspective, when the sociologist Max Weber (1864–1920) delivered 'Science as a vocation,' his famous address to graduate students embarking on academic careers, he stressed the subtle but real personal satisfaction one could derive from a life of scholarship, even knowing that one's work would be surpassed by future scholars.[43] Of course, Weber was assuming that scholarly work would be *read*. What was bold to assume in 1917 is merely false in 1997.

In the twentieth century, it has become popular for academics to see the pursuit of inquiry in Darwinian terms, whereby research is born into a world where survival depends on a process of critical scrutiny that resembles natural selection. It is expected that few pieces of research will survive intact across a variety of critical environments. But is this really the right metaphor? Would it not be truer to their epistemic predicament for scientists to say that most of today's research fails to survive because it perishes once it is published, stillborn, never quite connecting with an environment long enough for other scholars to subject it to critical scrutiny. (The grimness of this metaphor is meant to underscore that to be ignored is *not* to be subjected to a sophisticated form of criticism, the radical fantasies of humans to the contrary.)

As with so many of the other ailments of contemporary academic life, the natural sciences have displayed the most exaggerated symptoms, but the social sciences and humanities are following close on their heels. Credit for uncovering these symptoms in the 1960s belongs to Robert Merton and the historian Derek de Solla Price (1922–83). Unfortunately, they interpreted the emerging behemoth as representing the *health*, not the illness, of what Price called *Big Science*. It is a misdiagnosis from which humans continue to suffer, especially when they subject each other to peer evaluation. Merton, Price and their followers have gone to great lengths to portray organized enquiry as a massive industrial enterprise, but one that exhibits only its positive, not its negative, features. The most concrete symbol of their legacy is the *Science Citation Index* (*SCI*) and the attendant use of citation counts as indicators of quality, relevance, and influence. Few scientists can completely escape from thinking in these terms. The urge to measure one's career in terms of the droppings left at the foot and end of other people's articles is near irresistible.

The forty-year history of *SCI* is an object lesson in how the Knowledge Society works its insidious magic on unsuspecting intellectuals who come to believe they have taken control of the genie inhabiting a piece of information technology.[44] Shortly after the end of the Second World War, leading American scientists began to speak publicly of an 'explosion' or 'crisis' of information, which threatened to undermine scientific communication, the source of science's legendarily efficient division of labour. It seemed that scientists' lack of familiarity with the existing literature in their own fields was leading them to 'reinvent the wheel'. Initially the federal bureaucrats understood this inefficiency as pointing to a possible wastage of funds, but eventually they took it to signify a threat to national security, especially once the Soviet Union was shown to have a centralized scientific information network that made the non-duplication of existing effort a criterion for funding new proposals. Thus, what had been first presented as a problem for the individual scientist trying to sort out his or her research programme metamorphosed into a crisis in the unity of scientific knowledge itself.

Here it is worth noting the competing forces that drove the chemist, turned information scientist, Eugene Garfield, to design *SCI* as he did. On the one hand, Garfield was influenced by *Shepard's Citation Books*, which had been used by American lawyers and judges since 1873 to locate precedents for cases under trial. Each precedent was marked so as to indicate whether it supported or opposed the judgement of the case under consideration. The method served to integrate the body of legal knowledge by alerting legal practitioners of everything from the past that was available for them to draw upon. Consequently, once *Shepard's* was published, few cases went completely uncited in later legal decisions. On the other hand, Garfield was equally swayed by the enormousness of the scientific literature and the need to hire large numbers of relatively unskilled personnel to collect and codify the citations. His staff were thus in no position to read each article for the relationships in which citations stood to the literature they referenced. A strict numerical count of citations was all that could be managed under the circumstances. Nevertheless, these constraints on Garfield's labour force have had far-reaching consequences on the conclusions that both scholars and academic administrators have drawn from the patterns revealed in *SCI*, especially ones that all too easily translate indicators of quantity into ones of quality.

To appreciate these consequences, our Martian friends concentrate on the implicit logic of *SCI*'s citation counts, while ignoring the popular debating point of whether particular citations should be interpreted as crediting or discrediting the authors referenced. Officially, all citations are treated equally, as are all citers, or so it would seem. For, although *SCI* does not distinguish whether a given citer would, by other criteria, be regarded as a major or minor figure in the field, it does discriminate between someone who cites three works in an article and someone who cites thirty. The latter exerts ten times more influence over the final citation count than the former. This result is rather curious for an enterprise like science, which has been periodically advertised as the paradigm of democracy in action. In most democratic theories of voting, whenever one can vote for more than one candidate, the votes are treated as fractions adding up to one, so that each voter formally exerts the same influence over the electoral process, and voters with distributed allegiances are not privileged. However, the *SCI* counts enable authors who acknowledge a large number of scholarly debts – as measured by the citations they bestow on their colleagues – to exert disproportionate control over the structure of knowledge in their field. Imagine, if you will, a polity that by its electoral system discourages its citizens from being economically self-sufficient and ideologically focused. You will then appreciate the image of the scientific community implicitly promoted by *SCI*. (It sounds like a formula for producing the kind of 'dependency culture' that is the dark side of welfare state politics.)

Most democratic theories presume that voters cast their ballots fully realizing that their vote is a scarce resource: to give to one is to withhold from another. Of course, scholarly citation practices are no less strategic, but this fact is not registered in the way *SCI* counts citations. When each citation, but not each citer, is weighted equally, it becomes impossible to detect the deliberate enhancing or withholding of credit. Scientists would seem to cite simply because their knowledge claims demand that they do. The implied image of the citing scientist is one devoid of agency, which in turn creates the impression that a science is a spontaneously self-organizing field of activity that can be monitored as one would any other object of inquiry; hence, the expression *science of science*. Moreover, although *SCI* formally masks the strategic character of citing behaviour, once the citation counts are made public, the scientists can adjust their 'spontaneous' citing strategies. In a political system that enables one to cast a nonexclusive vote for a candidate, there will be a tendency to err on the side of voting beyond one's preferences, that is, to vote for every minimally acceptable candidate, so as to ensure that someone tolerable is elected. The corresponding tendency is for scientists to cite anyone who might have a hand in the fate of their article (or anyone whom such people would expect to see cited), lest the article be ignored and their next grant proposal go unfunded. We see, once again, Merton's fabulously mystified 'communist' ethic, which suggests that scientists cannot tell the difference between protection money and selfless sharing. Be that as it may, by adhering to this norm, scientists end up inflating the citation counts of their colleagues who are regarded as even marginally powerful, which in turn enhances the power of those colleagues, as *SCI* indicators are fed into the larger science policy process.

Soon after scientists started conspicuously using *SCI* to orient their research, science policy makers started using *SCI* to orient themselves to the scientists. Indeed, as an instrument of policy, *SCI* became an 'unobtrusive measure' of the pace and direction of scientific activity that worked to check scientists' own self-interested testimony on these matters. Policy makers can justify funding decisions that go against the wishes of the scientific community by arguing that they are merely trying to promote tendencies already present in *SCI* based indicators. In other words, actions that may appear disruptive at the local level of the individual scientist or research team reappear as supportive at the level of the 'knowledge system' that *SCI* based indicators are 'about'. The French postmodern philosopher, Jean Baudrillard (b. 1929), has coined the useful term *hyperreality* for a representation that, once extracted from the represented object, can be used as a standard against which to judge and shape that object, even though it is, strictly speaking, a fiction constructed by selectively attending to only some of the object's characteristics.[45] In that sense, the knowledge system is a hyperreal entity. To gauge the full sense of *SCI*'s impact, we need to go deeper and plumb the industrial unconscious of the Knowledge Society.

Price operationally defined 'science policy' as investment strategies for producing the largest number of highly cited articles.[46] He coupled this assumption with an interesting statistical fact: namely, that the clearest economic indicator of scientific productivity (as measured by number of papers published per scientist) is national energy consumption (as measured by kilowatt-hours per capita). Taken in gross terms, the coincidence was impressive. In the 1960s, the top ten producers of scientific knowledge were also the top ten consumers of electricity, with the USA accounting for 25 per cent of total production and 35 per cent of total consumption. Price then proceeded to treat this correlation as the basis for an analogy that has served to legitimate the indefinite and perhaps even profligate growth of scholarly production in all disciplines. Just as more customers can get cheaper electricity as the size of the power station increases, Price thought, so too a scaled up knowledge enterprise increases the likelihood that more scientists would produce citable papers, his measure of scholarly relevance and quality. The policy advice that followed was obvious: increase the number of people and effort devoted to the production of scholarly papers. Of course, the idea of channelling enormous talent in the single-minded pursuit of inquiry was not new. The most recent precedents for the idea's efficacy were to be found in the Second World War, when large numbers of academic natural scientists were sequestered in secret locations for the purpose of achieving a specific large outcome in a race against time; most notably, the atomic bomb. The successful campaign mounted by America's scientific elite to continue this model in peacetime has been widely documented.[47] However, the analogy that made the model attractive to Price in the first place has gone relatively unexamined.

The large scale utilities that so fascinated Price are efficient only in a very specific sense. Big plants produce more power but at a big cost to the environment, especially when measured in terms of the resources consumed by such plants that could have been used for other purposes, perhaps at another time. These are what economists call the 'opportunity costs' of producing energy in this so-called efficient manner. Ordinary folk experience the costs as pollution and waste. These observations apply equally to the fate of the people who are pumped into a scaled-up knowledge enterprise. As more of the highly cited articles are produced, the difference between the number of citations garnered by such articles and those garnered by all the other articles also increases, and there are, of course, more of those other uncited articles in the knowledge system. Once again, at the systemic level, policy makers hardly see this as cause for alarm. After all, it would seem to reveal the invisible hand of peer review miraculously discriminating important from unimportant research as the overall result of a set of privately taken decisions in referee's reports. But even sociologists of science who follow in the footsteps of Merton and Price find the disparity of cited and uncited articles to their advantage. Since highly cited articles in a field also tend to cross-reference each other, it is possible to construct an entire disciplinary narrative from the citation patterns of the 20–25 most highly cited articles.[48]

In the long term, larger knowledge enterprises produce more articles, by more people, that fail to be cited in the articles of those diminishing few whose articles are cited frequently. It is not uncommon in some fields for 90 per cent of the citations to go to 10 per cent of the authors. Here is a clear analogue of 'uneven development', whereby income disparities between rich and poor are aggravated in countries undergoing rapid industrialization. Indeed, these disparities become the basis for science's own version of class polarization, as the elite authors prove to be the most supportive of the use of *SCI* based indicators. Not surprisingly, then, sociologists of science unselfconsciously speak of the social stratification of science in terms reminiscent of world-systems theory: a 'core-set' of front-line scientists, on the one hand, and a 'peripheral' set of client-scientists, on the other.[49]

But the unevenness of scientific development has a temporal as well as a spatial dimension. For, in the world of Big Science, people who turn out to write highly cited articles are cited earlier in their careers, which suggests that the initial reception of these authors is strongly biased in terms of the academic networks they bring from graduate school. The *principle of cumulative advantage*, another of Merton's euphemisms, captures the idea that, as elsewhere in the industrial world, the rich get richer and the poor get poorer in the knowledge production business.[50] The *pièce de résistance* is the personal ideology that accompanies this uneven development, as scientists seem to believe that the knowledge system is ultimately just, with the really good ideas managing to survive even if their originators fade into oblivion. Merton even suggests that truly self-less scientists would turn over their best ideas to the people who they think will most likely draw attention to them. Needless to say, we have charted quite a perverted course from Weber's humble toiler in the groves of academe.

But suppose, our Martians imagine, one is among the few scientists who manage to keep their citation counts high. Consider the steady stream of ignorable articles that are dumped into the knowledge system. Their presence threatens to overwhelm one's ability to detect the few articles that are worth citing in one's own research. What can one do? As it turns out, the noise in the publication network can be avoided by adopting alternative forms of communication. Just as the rich are able to solve the problem of pollution to their personal satisfaction by moving to cleaner neighbourhoods, so too major scientists avoid the morass of journal literature by participating in *invisible colleges* that circulate work in prepublication form so as to enable relevant colleagues to get a head start on positioning their research programmes and grant proposals. Members of an invisible college also function as opinion leaders who influence the spin that less productive scientists give to the journal literature they read.[51]

In the natural sciences, the manoeuvres of these epistemic cartels have much of the character of insider trading in the stock market, where the stakes are very high indeed. Failure to equip one's laboratory with the right instruments and personnel within a limited amount of time can automatically eliminate the scientist from the cutting edge of research. More to the point, a failure to update one's research interests and skills in light of an ever shifting research frontier can consign even a highly cited scientist to the academic backwaters. A handy point of reference is the *SCI*-based indicator that bears Price's name. According to Price's Index, the 'harder' a science is perceived to be (where physics is the hardest science of them all), the lower the average age of the literature cited in its articles.[52] It would seem that, in the hard sciences, attention is just as difficult to sustain as it is to acquire. Science thus seems no exception to the rule that hard things are often the most brittle. Scientists have predictably adapted their careers to the accelerated pace of enquiry and the attendant planned obsolescence for scientific labour. Each new scientific growth area calls for the mastery of new knowledge, taking more experienced researchers further away from the intellectual capital they accumulated in graduate school. Rather than continuing to fight the uphill battle to remain in the front lines of research, scientists at ever earlier ages – nowadays in their early forties – shift over to the less technically demanding (though often equally stressful) work of full-time teaching or administration, for which they have received little or no training.[53]

Perhaps the most interesting effect of industrialized scientific knowledge production is what it does to the reading and writing habits of scientists. Citation practices provide, once again, the initial clue. In the hard sciences, if an article is frequently cited, it will be cited for the same reason, which is usually localizable to a particular section of the article: its theoretical framework; its review of the literature; its research methodology; its data; or its analysis of the data. By contrast, highly cited articles in the humanities and social sciences are cited for a variety of reasons in a variety of contexts.[54] Although the Martian anthropologists concede that it would be nice to believe that citation practices are stabilized in the hard sciences because their practitioners are converging on some objective reality, a much simpler hypothesis is that there are, as it were, fairly strong chains of interpretive command in those fields. Readers are specifically told to read certain articles for certain things that are worth emulating or attacking, and to ignore the rest. Consequently, an article's entire contribution may be stereotyped in terms of one of its parts, which can then be easily fitted into an ongoing disciplinary narrative. Of course, writing is affected by such reading practices, not least by an increasing reliance on *boilerplate*, those moveable modules of text that are sufficiently self-contained to appear anywhere in a given article and perhaps even in any article in a given field at a given time. Discussions of research methodology are perhaps most readily converted into boilerplate, but the onset of word processors has made virtually any part of an article susceptible to such treatment.

The result is a series of mass-produced articles, stitched to reveal enough seams to absolve readers of any guilt, were they to sample an article here and there but not read it in order of presentation, let alone in its entirety. It would seem that the disciplines that excel the most in the rigour of their methods and the reliability of their findings are also the ones that fail the most by the criteria that humanists respect: namely attention to the construction and reception of a text, including a thoughtfully critical response to the claims that the text makes. The fact that humanists have often managed to elicit surprising readings of scientific texts by treating them as works of literature or rhetoric merely reinforces the point that those texts are *not* normally read or even written to be read in that way.[55] But the way one treats texts is intimately tied to the way one treats their authors. The social ethic implicit in the careful readings valued by humanists are not matched by the treatment that scientific writings receive in the hands of the scientists themselves. The ease with which the sciences can yield to the rubrics of 'opinion leaders', 'spin control', 'boilerplate', 'planned obsolescence', and 'product life-cycles' vividly shows how the market mentality has penetrated the heartland of organized enquiry, rendering post-industrialism simply industrialism raised to the second order.[56] In fact *meta-industrialism* is a more apt expression than postindustrialism for science's epistemic plight, which all enquirers increasingly share.

The ultimate irony of *SCI*'s metamorphosis from postindustrial research tool to meta-industrial policy instrument is that scientists invited the move by their own image of self-contained communities of enquirers who are oriented exclusively towards each other. It follows that a summary of the judgements reached by such a body could be taken as a definitive record of its activities; in other words, *autonomy facilitated external control*. Because the humanities and social sciences are known to be routinely susceptible to forces beyond their control – such as the day's events, ambient ideologies, and public opinion – few have imagined that any neat set of unobtrusive measures could encapsulate their activities. Consequently, policy incursions into these 'soft sciences' have always appeared high-handed and messy, reflecting only one of many possible perspectives from which the development of these fields may be regarded. Therefore, it is truly perverse of celebrants of the Knowledge Society to declare that humanity is on the threshold of a new conception of knowledge that will have to be evaluated on its own emerging terms. After all, those terms emerged long ago, but are only now fully realizable. They can be summed up in the word *Positivism*; industrial society's final frontier.

Notes

1 Readers will recognize this literary technique as the one that Cervantes uses to frame *Don Quixote de la Mancha*. The only difference is that this is not a fiction. I actually was in the Harvard archives at that time, researching that book. Hopefully, by the time you read this, Fuller (1998), written under the Martian influence, will be in press. Needless to say, the book will exhibit many instances of that favourite Martian inference, 'abduction'!

2 Weinberg (1992) is one prominent physicist who seems to hold such a view.

3 Harding (1991).

4 Scientific heretics are easier to identify in the present than in the past because if their work is not eventually absorbed by orthodox science, they are typically recast as having been engaged in some non-scientific activity. Taylor (1996: 175–221) provides a good account of the cold fusion controversy as a recent scientific heresy. Other long-standing heresies, including psychokinesis and telepathy, are recounted in Hess (1993).

5 See, for example, Kitcher (1993).

6 This possibility originally appears as a thought experiment in Popper (1972).

7 MacKenzie (1995: 215–60).

8 Polanyi (1957).

9 Even if possible, would 'uninventing' nuclear bombs be such a good thing, if it also meant the extinction of the knowledge needed to disassemble old nuclear power plants? More generally, might nuclear weaponry be easier to control if its knowledge were routinized, so one could no longer be placed at the mercy of a 'mad scientist'? That was, after all, part of the motivation for 'testing' nuclear bombs.

10 Wittgenstein (1952).

11 Elster (1984).

12 Malinowski (1954).

13 Hollis and Lukes (1982).

14 Weber (1965).

15 Katz (1986).

16 Drucker (1993).

17 On the idea that science may suffer from 'diseconomies of scale' whereby more science increases our knowledge to a proportionally lesser degree than before, see Rescher (1984).

18 Tantalus, the source of the word 'tantalize', was a character in Greek mythology who was cursed with an unquenchable thirst, yet whenever he moved towards a juicy fruit, the wind blew the fruit out of his reach,

causing him to redouble his efforts, only to have the fruit elude him yet again. His torture thus consisted of being repeatedly frustrated just at the moment of consummation.

19 Fukuyama (1992).
20 Cohen (1994).
21 This observation is based on ongoing research comparing the labour market patterns of humanities, social science and natural science graduates in the UK. The principal investigators are Jane Fielding, Judith Glover and Deborah Smeaton of the University of Surrey. Needless to say, they are not committed to Martian inferences from their data.
22 Ben-David and Collins (1966).
23 Frank (1984).
24 Fuller (1997).
25 Turner and Chubin (1976).
26 For some background to assessing this counterfactual, see Inkster (1991: 32–59).
27 Even the principles of fixed-wing flight that underwrite the aeroplane had been developed by an aristocratic amateur, George Cayley (1773–1857), upon whose ideas the Wright brothers improved by trial and error. On the independence of engineering from physics as a body of knowledge, see Vincenti (1990).
28 McCloskey (1983).
29 Brown (1984).
30 Hull (1988) and Kitcher (1993).
31 Feyerabend (1979).
32 Bell (1982) provides a good brief analysis of the social processes of secularization.
33 Latour (1987).
34 MacIntyre (1970).
35 Merton (1973: 267–78).
36 Metaphysically speaking, this shift amounts to the difference between regarding science as a *universal* that may be instantiated in any of a variety of social environments (Merton's view) and regarding it as already an integral *part* of one such environment (the Martian view). On the significance of going from a universal-particular to a whole-part metaphysics for understanding science, see Fuller (1996a).
37 Mulkay (1990: 62–78).
38 Holmes and McLean (1990: 146–70).
39 Raj (1988).
40 Collins (1985).
41 Chubin and Hackett (1990: 85–91).
42 Bell (1973).
43 Weber (1958).

44 Here the Martians draw on the ongoing research of Wouters (1994).
45 Baudrillard (1983).
46 Price (1978).
47 Kleinman (1995).
48 Small (1975).
49 Pinch (1990).
50 Merton (1973: 439–59).
51 Price (1986)
52 Price (1970).
53 Merton (1973: 497-559).
54 Cozzens (1985).
55 Bazerman (1987).
56 De Mey (1982: 111–72).

5

The Secret of Science's Success: Convenient Forgetfulness

Recovering science's historicity: Needham's Grand Question

A sense of *historicity* is essential for understanding the grip that science has had on the global imagination. I mean here something more than just an awareness of the temporal ordering of achievements that have been made in the name of Western science. By 'historicity' I mean the way in which one's perception of what has transpired in the history of science shapes one's sense of the prospects for future developments. The tricky thing about getting to grips with the historicity of science is that it typically involves examining the long term consequences of people acting on the basis of profoundly false beliefs about the history of science. While it is now widely conceded that the most pervasive accounts of the history of science – those found in science textbooks and science popularizations – are misleading to the point of being self-serving, few have stepped back to wonder what this might mean for an activity that advertises itself as unique in its quest for some ultimate, singular and unified truth.

For their part, scientists, often aided by obliging philosophers, have gone into a state of denial over this matter, arguing that if our historical understanding of science were indeed so flawed, then 'we' (mostly Westerners) would not be enjoying our current high state of civilization. However, these scientists are often the first to admit that their world-historic predecessors – Newton, Maxwell, Einstein, etc. – did not fully fathom the consequences of their world-shattering ideas and, given the chance, would perhaps disown the consequences that we now consider to have earned them their place in the scientific pantheon. From the perspective of scientists who make such arguments, it seems epistemologically safer to say that their precursors failed to see into the future than that they themselves have failed to see into the past. Thus, time and truth are made to move in the same direction – forward. No definition of *progress* could be more to the point. In a sense, little more than an exercise in semantics is at stake in trying to distinguish between, say, Newton's misunderstanding of the long-term significance of a truth he uttered 300 years ago and the latest Nobel Prize winner's attribution of contemporary significance to a statement that he falsely believes Newton to have made 300 years ago. Nevertheless, as will become clear in the rest of this book, the reinforcement of this subtle shift in the burden of error from the present to the past – between regarding the history of science as a series of, so to speak, *our realized falsehoods* and *their unrealized truths* – is crucial for representing the sense of superiority that science is thought to confer on the West.

For example, a broad spectrum of philosophers of science have believed that the 'best explanation' of science's success lies in the fact that its most recent theories account for things better than earlier ones did. These philosophers invite us to imagine scientists' attempts to describe and explain bits of reality as a kind of linguistic archery, in which science's aim at the essence of things grows better with practice over time. (Our Martian friends of the previous chapter would immediately recognize this as the military side of the military–industrial metaphor.) The 'theory of reference' in philosophy is largely given over to such considerations. However, the superficial plausibility of the archery analogy starts to fade, once we consider that all the 'contestants' are not present at the same match. Indeed, the more closely we look at the history, the more we see that our scientific contestants were probably not even playing the same game. Step back for a moment and ask the following questions which challenge our everyday sense of the history of science. How many of the people responsible for the exemplary achievements of Western science would have approved of the directions in which their work has subsequently been taken? Would they even have been comfortable with the specific role they have been assigned in popular renditions of the progressive march towards the Truth? More specifically, would Aristotle, and Darwin, for that matter, appreciate being seen as landmark figures in a science, biology, that has increasingly reformulated its problems and insights in terms that shift the locus of investigation from the observation of nature to the manufacture of experimental effects?

Nevertheless, while the rhetorical force of these questions may be lethal for 'best explanation' accounts of the success of science, the avenues of enquiry they open up should not really surprise us. After all, the faultiness of human memory, biases of the written record, and the tendency for words to change meanings as they move across contexts all conspire to render any straightforwardly progressive account of the history of Western science patently false, yet also difficult to falsify. This paradoxical state of affairs is enhanced as our liabilities gravitate towards our interests: in a phrase, the fine art of *convenient forgetfulness*. As we shall see in what follows, much of the historiography of science can be discussed in terms of who is and is not convenienced by a particular strategy of forgetting. An important part of this story is inscribed in the disciplinary difference between those who do science and those who engage in 'second-order' studies of how science is done. The latter group includes students of the history, philosophy, sociology, psychology, political economy – and so forth – of science. Taken as a group, with the exception of most of the philosophers, they draw attention to the fallible features of the human condition that, by implication, render the narrative of progress recounted in science textbooks little more than a myth. Practitioners of these second-order fields typically welcome their professional separation from the scientific fold because of its liberation from the scrutiny of scientists worried about how an altered view of the past might affect their legacy to future scientists. However, there is a downside to this hard-won autonomy, especially in the case of historians of science. Not only are they no longer bothered by scientists, they are ignored altogether, as scientists have virtually stopped appealing to the past to justify contemporary concerns, except in *purely* mythical terms, as in 'The Leap of Thales', to quote a chapter title of one recent popularization.[1]

It is important to point out that this was not always the case. Many of the people responsible for drawing attention to original archival materials in the history of science at the end of the nineteenth century were such distinguished scientists as Ernst Mach (1838–1916), Pierre Duhem (1861–1916), and Wilhelm Ostwald (1853–1932). They used these materials against colleagues who championed the dominant research programmes of their day. The common strategy of these historically minded scientists was to show that whatever empirical successes could be credited to the dominant programmes were offset by conceptual problems that were never adequately addressed when first posed, often several centuries earlier but since then conveniently forgotten.[2] It may now seem quixotic for the late philosopher Feyerabend to have cited Aristotle's metaphysical conception of motion – which included both locomotion and organic change under the same rubric – as a strike against the disciplinary distinction between physics and biology, yet such a move would have had a sympathetic hearing from Duhem and Ostwald, both of whom favoured the concept of 'energy' as a move back to Aristotle's unified vision. Indeed, these scientists spoke for the past much as environmentalists today to speak for 'future generations' in their attempt to divert their contemporaries from potentially destructive courses of action. Given the argument that the past is no longer relevant to the present, they observed that problems do not necessarily disappear simply because they are forgotten. The collective memory trace is still there to be activated.

This is the spirit in which the half-century study of Chinese science conducted by the late embryologist Joseph Needham (1900–95) should be seen. Needham devoted eight thick volumes of original scholarship to fathoming why China's clear political, economic, and even technological advantage over Europe did not materialize in a 'scientific revolution' comparable to the one that is thought to have been responsible for propelling Europe forward.[3] When compared with the critiques of Mach, Duhem and Ostwald, Needham's had a depth that (one might say) corresponded to his removal from the day-to-day conduct of science. Although Needham's message is not as clear as one might like it to have been, the general tenor of his lifework was to highlight the *contingent* character of the West's scientific ascendency; that is, science as the West has come to know and value it may be only a transitory feature of the human condition.

Needham posed a self-styled 'Grand Question': *Why did the Scientific Revolution not take place in China?* There are two subtly different ways of interpreting it that have profound implications for both how one goes about answering the question and what one takes to be the larger significance of the question. One reading presumes that the Revolution would happen unless it were explicitly blocked, whereas the other presumes that it would not happen unless it were explicitly promoted. Since Needham himself seemed to play off both interpretations, it becomes especially important that we highlight the distinction between what are, respectively, *overdeterminationist* and *underdeterminationist* interpretations of the Grand Question.[4]

On the one hand, one may suppose that a 'Scientific Revolution' inevitably happens to human beings everywhere, once a certain critical mass of 'social intelligence' has been reached: that is, unless a locally occurrent factor prevents it. According to this overdeterminationist view of history, one would not necessarily expect China to have produced exactly the same conditions that led to the Scientific Revolution in the West, but only functionally equivalent conditions, as constructed from China's own cultural and material resources. For example, instead of the Greek natural philosophy tradition, Needham pointed to Taoism as having provided comparable cultural precedent. Here the comparison of European and Chinese science can be seen as a kind of 'controlled experiment' to isolate the factors that enabled the mathematical-experimental sciences to take off in seventeenth-century Europe but not in China. History simulates laboratory conditions. Europe and China were sufficiently isolated from one another for, where comparable precedents failed to produce identical results, the inhibiting factor to be intrinsic to the culture, and not a product of any cross-cultural interaction.

The overdeterminationist position largely captures the historiographical sensibility of practicing scientists. It envisages that the universality of science is represented historically in terms of several culturally distinct lines of inquiry gradually converging on a common epistemic trajectory. Thus, the overdeterminationist is prone to look for 'multiple' or 'simultaneous' discoveries of the same scientific phenomenon. Because all cultures have the potential to reach the same conclusions, it follows that a value can be placed on being the first to arrive at an intellectual destination that many others seek. But, for the very same reason, the overdeterminationist does not regard cultures as the unique possessors of scientific ideas in any literal sense that would entail the assignment of intellectual property rights. In all these respects, the overdeterminationist is one with eighteenth-century Enlightenment thought about science as a universal form of knowledge.

On the other hand, the underdeterminationist, more a creature of the early nineteenth-century Romantic mentality, comes closer to the professional historian's sensibility. Here Needham's question is interpreted to mean that the Scientific Revolution was a unique event in the history of the West that occurred only because certain culturally specific conditions obtained. This revolutionary moment subsequently acquired its global significance, not through independent rediscovery but by the West's active intervention in the affairs of non-Western cultures. In other words, China was never in a 'race' to reach the revolutionary moment, notwithstanding the superficial similarities in its cultural trajectory with that of the West. This is more in the general spirit of Needham's project, which is organized more around a holistic understanding of Chinese civilization than an equally in-depth comparative history of Chinese and European science. It is also the interpretation presumed by the Sinologist Nathan Sivin, who then criticized Needham's lapses into over-determinationism, as when Needham infers a failure on China's part from a simple difference in outcome between it and the West.[5] According to Sivin's diagnosis, whenever Needham marvelled at why the revolution did not take place in China, he seemed to be focusing on intellectual factors to the exclusion of social ones. At the same time, it might be claimed that Needham's 'lapses' into overdeterminationism were simply an expression of his approval of the West's Scientific Revolution as a desirable intellectual destination, at least when it occurred, if not in all of its subsequent developments.[6]

Considered from an epistemological perspective, the choice between underdeterminationist and overdeterminationist historiographies may depend on what needs to be explained. The former is better suited to explain the singular emergence of science, the latter to its spread once it has been introduced. In his underdeterminationist moments, Needham cast his thesis in terms of historically contingent social factors which ensured that the rise of science appeared neither miraculous nor racially grounded, two interpretations he strenuously disavowed. But in that case, history must be only moderately underdetermined, for the more necessary a particular historical trajectory appears to have been for the rise of science, the less probable the revolution's actual occurrence then becomes. In other words, for Needham's claims about his own achievement to make sense, it must have been historically possible for the Scientific Revolution to have happened in Europe in a way other than it actually did. Needham himself suggests as much when observing that the social preconditons for the general testing of speculative hypotheses by technological means (the essence of the experimental method) had been in place as far back as the thirteenth century, when the first European universities were chartered as corporate entities on the model of guilds. This formal equality in the legal status of academics and craftsmen made commerce between them much easier than in the more class-segregated societies of the East, which presumably helped seed the academic imagination with thoughts for how their speculations could be materially realized. In that case, the question is opened: could the Scientific Revolution have occurred somewhat earlier than it did, given that the crucial precondition had already been in place for nearly five centuries?

But if history could have gone otherwise at too many junctures, then none of these 'turning points' could serve as genuine crossroads, in the sense of a set of outcomes that are more or less uniquely determined by the road chosen at one point. The reason is that each fork on the road would then simply be an invitation to encounter other forks later on. For example, the rhetorical power of the most influential recent work of social history of science, *Leviathan and the Air-Pump*,[7] rests on the assumption that the debate between Robert Boyle and Thomas Hobbes over the validity of experimental knowledge was the *only* major turning point in the history of Western science, with the subsequent 350 years being little more than a ratification of the experimentalist perspective championed by Boyle. Much of the force of the authors' argument would have been subverted, had they tried to explain why it took another two or more centuries after Boyle's alleged victory for the experimental sciences to find a regular place in the Western university curriculum, since they would then have to reintroduce many 'Hobbesian' considerations that Boyle had supposedly suppressed for good. Thus, as we saw in Chapter 3, experimentation had to be reinvented as the source of empirical checks on an essentially theory- (or paradigm-) driven enterprise that, by the end of the nineteenth century, had come to epitomize the spirit of critical rationalism celebrated by university culture and largely championed by Hobbes.

Metahistory	Overdetermined	Underdetermined
Whose perspective?	Today's scientist	Past scientist
History's natural tendency	Convergence upon one end	Divergence to multiple ends
Key to history	'Rationality'	'Turning points'
Extreme version	Inevitabilism ('All cultures eventually become scientific')	Indeterminism ('It's a miracle that any culture became scientific')
Likelihood that a Scientific Revolution would occur	High	Low
What needs to be explained about the Scientific Revolution?	How it was disabled (in China)	How it was enabled (in Europe)

Figure 5.1 Two metahistories of science.

Here overdeterminationism comes into its own, specifically, as an explanation of the apparent *irreversibility* (often read as the 'universality') of the spread of the Western conception of science. The standard overdeterminationist appeal to science's patent 'rationality' as a motive force is meant to mediate between the extremes of *innatism* and *imperialism:* that is, between explaining the spread of science in terms of humanity's natural susceptibility to the scientific world-view, on the one hand, and the sheer political power of the imperial carriers of that world-view, on the other. In this way, non-Westerners are rehabilitated as more or less voluntary collaborators in the Western scientific project. But the plausibility of this story starts to be stretched once it seems that any culture, regardless of its epistemic history, can converge on *the* scientific trajectory associated with the West. How can something so powerful *not* exact substantial costs from its various host cultures? One perennial answer, nowadays associated with Francis Fukuyama, traces science's cross-cultural translatability to its underwriting of the technological know-how needed for a society to be an efficient engine of wealth creation.[8] With this view, science's vaunted 'universality' comes from it being a necessary means to universally desired ends, the price for which all societies will gladly pay in terms of making the requisite cultural adaptations (i.e. 'eliminating error'). Of course, the alternative story is that science transforms all things in the course of subserving them to its own imperatives. 'Autonomous science' would thus acquire the sinister connotations that the social critic Langdon Winner has attached to 'autonomous technology', that great leveller of all cultural difference and spiritual integrity.[9] We shall return to this set of issues in the next chapter, when considering the Islamic and Japanese responses to science's ascendency in the West.

Temporal colonialism: a retrospected past and an irreversible future

Even if we grant this division of explanatory labour between the two metahistories, another question remains. How does one account for 'pre-scientific' forms of knowledge? Here we can find a backward-looking form of overdeterminationism: a *retrospective colonization of the past*. It implies that one has not gained legitimate access to, say, a form of technological knowledge unless the scientific principles on which the technology is 'based' have been mastered. If this 'basis' historically appeared after the technology was already developed and used, the proposal amounts to systematically disempowering the users and then reacquainting them with their artifacts by means of theory-driven instruction. This is not an idle possibility, but in fact a pattern has been noted historically in the 'scientization' of the professions, as craft based training in medicine and engineering yielded to academic certification. It can also be seen in efforts to Westernize Third World curricula for purposes of rendering the natives 'governable' by making them epistemically accountable to standards that Western authorities can understand and evaluate.

An especially insidious context of native disempowerment occurs when Europeans rewrite the histories of non-European peoples who are no longer around to criticize the histories reconstructed on their behalf. Take the Incan settlement at Machu Picchu, Peru, which archaeologists now believe to have been an agricultural station devoted to the effects of different soils on crop yield.[10] The level of soil discrimination evidenced at Machu Picchu remained unmatched by the combined efforts of botanists and chemists in Europe until the mid-nineteenth century. Indeed, European scientists had not been driven to acquire agricultural knowledge with the Incan eye for detail until potatoes imported from the

Americas helped eliminate many nutritional disorders in Europe. This lengthened lifespan, which, coupled with a constant fertility rate, led to an increase in the rate of population growth. Under the circumstances, it became important for Europeans not simply to grow more potatoes and kindred crops, but to determine how crop yields could be increased per unit of arable land. Experimental investigations along these lines had clearly been undertaken at Machu Picchu five centuries earlier. However, because the Incas demonstrated their agricultural knowledge 'merely' in experimental practice, and not as deductions from any recognized principles of natural science, Europeans have tended to downgrade the Incan contributions as 'pre-theoretical', 'trial and error' ('inductive', if one is being especially polite), or 'technology' (as opposed to 'science'). Each of these expressions is meant to suggest that had the Incas 'really' understood what they were up to, they would have eventually arrived at the theories of agronomy that we now regard as providing the best explanation for the level of agricultural success they achieved.

Once again, we see the calling card of overdeterminationism, namely, the assumption that all genuine knowledge eventually converges on the same trajectory – 'ours'. It used to be claimed that a symptom of the Incas' lack of scientific understanding was that they did not exploit opportunities for extending their knowledge in ways that 'we' would have done under comparable circumstances. However, as military history has come to be fitted into the history of science, Europeans have reluctantly admitted that their own conquistador-like urges may have contributed to the Incas' failure to extend their agricultural knowledge beyond a certain point. A still bolder, more underdeterminationist hypothesis is that the Incas had a radically different sense of the social role of knowledge in their world, one that the visiting Europeans could not readily grasp, given their lack of schooling even in their own scientific traditions. For example, the fact that the Incas lacked a sense of the cosmos unified under a creative deity could count as prima facie evidence for their world-view being radically different from that of the Europeans. But such speculation aside, historians today have no trouble asserting that when it came to acquiring the Incas' degree of agricultural sophistication, European scientists were at a distinct disadvantage, given the Western tradition of treating plants as degenerate animals and biochemical changes as 'emergent' on underlying physical processes. This is simply to say that agriculture significantly deviated from the paradigm of Western scientific inquiry, mathematical physics.

Nevertheless, its political correctness notwithstanding, if we dogmatically stress the radical differences between Incan and European modes of thought, it then becomes just as difficult to *credit* the Incas for having 'anticipated' European agricultural science as to discredit them for not actually having invented modern agronomy. This problem becomes especially acute once we consider forms of identity politics that turn on a culture's possession of a privileged, or at least distinct, form of knowledge. If the culture is not careful, its efforts at establishing epistemic autonomy can easily turn into epistemic isolation. Good contemporary examples of contrasting strategies for dealing with the problem can be found among *feminists* and *Afrocentrists*.[11] They represent, respectively, an underdeterminationist and overdeterminationist approach to the identity politics of science.

Feminists often stress alternative ways of doing science, ones based on intuition, empathy, caring and other 'subjective' modes of epistemic access that have been routinely devalued by the male European scientific tradition. At their most utopian, they envision a day in which scientific practice will be transformed by the leadership of enlightened women and feminist men, perhaps even at the very earliest stages of socialization, as boys are reared to relate to the world with the same degree of receptiveness to the standpoint of 'the other' as girls typically are.[12] However, there is a crucial ambiguity as to the exact identity of this utopia. Does it simply involve according subjectivity the dominant role traditionally reserved for objectivity, or is some sort of dialectical synthesis in the offing? A complicating factor is that the subjective mode associated with women's experience is neither exclusive to women (consider such 'pre-feminist' male defenders of intuition as Saint Augustine and Saint Bonaventure, Schelling, Bergson, and Polanyi) nor perhaps even a distinct form of experience in its own right. In the latter case, I mean to suggest the possibility that the historical emergence of a gendered division of labour – the 'head' versus the 'heart', so to speak – has produced complementary forms of alienation for men and women. From that standpoint, to call for the replacement of objectivizing modes of experience with subjectivizing ones is a bit like saying that the cure for sadism is masochism.

In other words, a close examination of all the claims that have been advanced on behalf of intuition as a source of knowledge in the history of the West would reveal that they do not share much more than an interest in compensating for the inadequacy of discursive forms of knowledge. Moreover, given the many centuries in which a gendered division of labour has shaped a bifurcated consciousness in human beings, it should not be assumed that the reintegration of the masculine and feminine poles would constitute a return to an 'Edenic' unified human psyche. Given these uncertainties about the exact character of a feminist scientific utopia, it is understandable that the practical politics of feminist science have gravitated towards more procedurally democratic claims for proportional gender representation in the scientific workplace, which renders any change in consciousness primarily an emergent feature of this institutional reform.

In contrast, Afrocentrists envision a day in which Africans will finally be given credit for discoveries that Europeans have so far claimed for themselves. Here we find the rhetoric of the 'stolen legacy'.[13] Yet for all its surface harshness, Afrocentrist rhetoric presupposes that the Africans and Europeans have basically the *same* scientific legacy, one whose African precedents the Europeans refuse to acknowledge. Sometimes this refusal is traced back to the Greeks themselves, whose mercantile practices abroad are interpreted as cultural theft by Afrocentrist scholars. A more historically nuanced charge is associated with the 'Black Athena' thesis of Martin Bernal, who argues that Prussian philologists manufactured a Greek origin to European culture in order to complement Napoleon's appropriation of ancient Rome as France's heroic mythical ancestor.[14] As the concept of 'race' scientifically hardened over the course of the nineteenth century, the Greeks were made into the source of the 'Aryan' race whose inherent cultural superiority is still signalled whenever someone today remarks on 'how much further' a Greek was able to take a concept or technique that originated in the Near East, India, or Egypt.

Nevertheless, it would seem that, compared with the Afrocentrists, the feminists are charting the more ambitious agenda, one which goes beyond redressing past injustices and moves towards a genuinely alternative science. The few cases of Afrocentric inquiry in which Africans supposedly enjoyed epistemic access to something that has completely eluded European science probably constitute the most contested area of Afrocentric scholarship. A case in point is the so-called 'Melanin Hypothesis,' which ascribes special psychic powers to the skin colour of pre-colonial Africans.[15] Even committed Africanists often find it a little too convenient to hold European invaders responsible for preventing Africans from transmitting their pigment based knowledge to future generations. Rather, the difference in the visionary scope of feminists and Afrocentrists is best explained as a reflection of a difference in their perception of the prospects for a political change that would benefit their respective constituencies in the present day. The feminists are more optimistic than the Afrocentrists that we can collectively move to a radically reformed world. Afrocentrists would seem to be willing to settle for a share of the credit for what has already been accomplished in the name of the West.

Whatever is ultimately made of the political and intellectual merits of Afrocentrism, it deserves credit for drawing critical attention to the forward looking perspective that is taken for granted by the overdeterminationists' philosophical cousins, those devotees of linguistic archery to whom we alluded early in this chapter: the *scientific realists*.[16] For example, why do we automatically say that Africans, Incans, or some other non-Western peoples 'unconsciously anticipated' Western scientific discoveries? Why not say, instead, that Westerners have merely recovered or explicated the insights originally gleaned by the Africans or Incans, which, because they were too organically integrated in their lifestyles – 'second nature', so to speak – did not require any explicit articulation in their culture? As we have seen in the case of the melanin scholars, the second nature can be literally inscribed on the epidermis itself. Such a historical orientation is no less 'realist' than that of the philosophies of science that usually travel under that rubric, except for the fact that it locates the sought-after reality in the *past* rather than in the present (and future) state of science.

If we have become overly accustomed to envisaging disparate inquiries gradually converging on an ultimate theory of reality, we may need to recall an alternative vision, one often adumbrated by Afrocentrist and some feminist rhetoric: namely, that there was a Golden Age in the distant past, followed by something like the Biblical fall from grace, from which we are now only slowly recovering. Indeed, according to this view, a premier sign of our 'fallen' state is that we require specialized discourses that are alienated from the normal run of life in order to capture what the Africans, Incans, etc., were able to embody in practices that were integrated into their daily lives. And lest one dismiss this vision as tainted by a naive romanticism, it is worth recalling that this was largely the West's own sense of history until the middle of the eighteenth century. The key notion here is what the Renaissance Humanists called *prisca sapientia*, or 'pristine wisdom', which justified the reading of ancient Greek and Hebrew texts in their original – and presumably uncorrupted – languages. In the hands of the Protestant Reformers, this became a potent weapon for challenging the religious authority of the Roman Catholic Church and the intellectual authority of its Scholastic teachers, who preferred a homogenized Latin tongue (much as English would be preferred today by professional academics as the melting pot for cultural differences). But perhaps the most striking case of the persistence of the belief in *prisca sapientia* is Isaac Newton's lifelong attempt to locate precedents for his physical discoveries in the Bible, the pre-Socratic philosopher Pythagoras, and the Hermetic corpus of Egypt.[17]

But, given the endurance of the idea of a *prisca sapientia*, when did the West acquire its characteristically forward-looking view of where the secrets of reality lay? The answer may be found in the complicated history surrounding the *Battle of the Books*. This battle, so-named by the Irish satirist and cleric Jonathan Swift (1667–1745), transpired mostly in Britain and France over the entire stretch of the Enlightenment (roughly 1650–1800). Sometimes it is said that the two sides of the dispute – the *ancients* and the *moderns* – were contesting the relative merits of ancient (i.e. Greek and Latin) and modern (i.e. English and French) literature, although neither side denied the goodness of the ancient classics.

A better clue to the nature of the dispute is the origin of the distinction between 'ancient' and 'modern' starting in the late thirteenth century, when the Scholastics wrangled over the adequacy of Aristotle's syllogistic approach to logic, which required that one suppose the existence of whatever one reasoned about. Here the 'via antiqua' stood for a defence of Aristotle's logic, whereas the 'via moderna', championed by the arch-sceptic William of Ockham (c.1285–c.1349), stood for those who wanted to adopt a proposition based logic, one whose major premises would be formulated as hypotheses rather than straightforward existence claims. In other words, the moderns did not want to commit to the truth of the premisses from which they argued before deriving their logical consequences. This detachment of substantive truth from formal validity became characteristic of the ironic stance of the Scholastics at the end of the Middle Ages. On the one hand, it enabled them to entertain the possibility of a heliocentric universe and inertial motion, both of which contradicted the received word of Aristotle but was eventually vindicated by Galileo; on the other hand, it also prevented them from committing to the truth of these hypotheses.

Similarly, in the Battle of the Books, the ancients held that the literatures of the West's founding cultures contained original truths that cannot be reduced to a formula or method whose structure later texts can elucidate. Rather, the contemporary reader simply needs to become sensitive to the subtlety of ancient expression in order to appreciate its natural superiority. In contrast, the moderns argued that the idiosyncrasies of the ancient texts are little more than that, and are therefore best taken as imperfect expressions of ideas that can be brought out more clearly today and even more so tomorrow, as we hypothesize what the ancient authors meant to say and then, using evidence unavailable to them, try to say it better ourselves. At the limit, the modern would replace all the ancient texts with contemporary ones that transcended the limits, while preserving the best, of their precursors.

This 'later is better' mentality marks the difference between scientific attitudes towards writing and broadly *hermeneutical* attitudes that encompass not only the secular classics but more importantly, from a cross-cultural perspective, the religious ones as well.[18] If the scientist sees past texts as rough drafts of future ones, the hermeneutician sees future texts as pale copies of the originals. It is worth noting that by the mid-nineteenth century, the Battle of the Books had reached the point of literary critics wondering whether modernism taken to its logical conclusion might altogether dissolve the very presumption of historical continuity between past and present texts, thereby reducing literary legitimacy to a function of immediate social context.[19] While this sentiment drove an increasingly large wedge between the critics and practitioners of the arts (with the critics retaining the sense of historical continuity and artists obscuring it), the sciences largely refused to take the next step into what we now call *postmodernism*.

The method of modernist metahistory: time-discounting

The modernist rewriting of the past as the anticipation of the present is crucial for explaining a feature of Western culture that has often been held responsible for the rise of science. Fortified by the original science policy shaman, Britain's Lord Chancellor Francis Bacon (1561–1626), Western inquirers did not fear any backlash effect from their experimental attempts to bend nature to their collective will. Psychologically speaking, such organized fearlessness is most easily maintained under two conditions.

1 The inquirers themselves do not need to live with the consequences of their actions (perhaps because these occur in remote times and places, as in the case of environmental hazards).
2 History is rewritten to such an extent that by the time these consequences occur, they will seem to have been what were desired all along.

These two conditions can be summed up as the systematic conversion of a psychic liability into a virtue. It is the phenomenon that economists call *time-discounting*, or simply *discounting*, whereby people prefer the satisfaction of immediate desires to distant ones, even if the distant ones are likely to be greater, and the satisfaction of the immediate desires may jeopardize the satisfaction of the distant ones.[20] A simple example is overweight people who gorge themselves on food now, although it undermines their long-term interest in losing weight.

There are two schools of thought on whether or not discounting is rational. Welfare economics presupposes the patent irrationality of discounting. Accordingly, the function of the state is to compensate for the human tendency to exaggerate the longevity of our immediate interests which leads us to discount the future too heavily.[21] Compensation is provided by progressive taxation, social security insurance and other schemes to redistribute income, as well as incentives to invest rather than consume. Indeed, in his classic *A Theory of Justice* (1971), John Rawls (b. 1921) raised this counter-discounting sensibility to a philosophical verity: that is, the best way to motivate a sense of social justice is by persuading agents that, at some point in their lives, they may end up in *anyone*'s current situation, so they should not treat their present position, however favourable, as indefinitely extendable into the future.[22] When forced to decide from behind such a 'veil of ignorance', power relationships metamorphose into epistemic ones: when I accept a certain income redistribution scheme, I am not so much manipulating other people's lives as rationally planning for a prospect that may well become my own (e.g. the expectation of my eventual retirement). Consequently, one is placed in a frame of mind whereby the strong proprietary distinction among selves dissolves into an undifferentiated sense of social belonging.[23] But for all its admirable qualities, had the welfare mentality successfully pervaded all spheres of activity in the West, it is unlikely that the 'fearlessness' attributed to the Scientific Revolution would have ever been manifested.

This last observation suggests that we may not do justice to discounters by reducing their world-view to the mistaken induction that one's immediate desires will continue in perpetuity. Rather, discounters should perhaps be given credit for the meta-level realization that it is precisely this propensity for preferring the temporally near to the temporally far that will continue in perpetuity. In that case, by the time people reach the point at which they should regret their earlier decisions, the consequences of those decisions will have shaped what they now desire, thereby turning regret into acceptance, if not outright endorsement, as in the case of the phenomena associated with that complement of 'sour grapes', the phenomenon of *sweet lemons*.[24] Thus, overweight people who continue eating and thereby fail to curb their obesity in the long term may eventually come to devalue the significance of achieving a 'normal' weight.

In other words, discounting is a rational strategy if one believes that the past is just as constructible as the future, or, as the French political sociologist Raymond Aron (1905–83) so elegantly put it, 'The past is never definitively fixed except when it has no future'.[25] Such a sensibility gives the overdeterminationist history of science its plausibility because, somewhat paradoxically, the idea that reality has a deep, invariant structure to which our access may nevertheless improve over time presupposes that, if need be, we can discount long-standing beliefs in favour of a recent discovery, whose significance is sufficiently deep that we can imagine that it would have been recognized as such by our intellectual ancestors, had they stumbled upon it. Indeed, this argument was used to great effect by Galileo Galilei (1564–1642) in response to the Jesuits who wondered why, if his astronomical findings were true, they had not been registered by the Biblical patriarchs or Church fathers. The answer was that they never had the opportunity to look through a telescope – but had they, they would, presumably, have been drawn to Galileo's conclusion.

Although many cultures have had elaborate literary recording practices, one increasingly prominent tendency in Europe set it apart as a culture ripe for the collective discounting of historical memory illustrated by both Galileo's response to the Jesuits and the retrospective colonization of the past noted in the previous section. That tendency – much to the consternation of the Roman Catholic Church – was the relatively uncontrolled production and distribution of printed materials.[26] Most commentators on the signficance of the printing press for the Scientific Revolution have focused on the sheer availability of books as making it unnecessary for new authors to summarize received wisdom before setting out their own contributions.[27] One could simply presume that readers had access to earlier works and then devote one's energies almost exclusively to one's own novel findings or conceptions. In this way, the pace of intellectual progress quickened. However, at least as important was the fact that books were disseminated from many different sources that often contradicted one another, especially in their characterization of the past and its legacy for the present. This simultaneous proliferation of texts erased any clear temporal source of knowledge. In this way, the continual rewriting of the past to serve present needs became a matter of implicit practice, if not official doctrine. Although it is common nowadays to associate scepticism about the search for historical origins with the work of Foucault, Derrida, and other postmodern thinkers, such scepticism was already present in the early modern period – for example, in the popularity of self-consciously mythical 'philosophical history' during the Enlightenment. Indeed, as the elusiveness of the spatio-temporal coordinates of the West's Scientific Revolution continues to illustrate, even today relatively few branches of history are underpinned by an incontrovertible chronology.

As the great German philosopher Hegel (1770–1831) first realized when pondering exactly who or what could have a 'history', the establishment of canonical historical trajectories has required substantial state intervention, typically involving the mass indoctrination of students in state-sanctioned school textbooks. Not surprisingly, political history has been most susceptible to this treatment, in which the familiar litany of dates of particular leaders, treaties and battles serves to underscore the legitimacy of the current regime. Indeed, it is often forgotten that the advent of professional historical scholarship, especially its reliance on period documents as the main evidentiary base for historical claims, coincided with the rise of what is known as *Whig history*; the form of overdeterminationism whereby the past lends its weight in support of present-day entitlement claims. The connection, as the young Lord Acton observed, is that heavy documentation interpreted in one's favour creates a burden of proof against any attempt to challenge the legitimacy of one's rule.[28]

However, in the West, this practice has to be set against the backdrop of an increasingly democratic political process, one which encourages contesting parties to revise continually the relative significance assigned to the dates in the textbook chronologies, as well as the national goals they are meant to serve. The most famous programmatic statement of the sociology of knowledge, *Ideology and Utopia* (1929), by Karl Mannheim (1893–1947), can be read in this context, one in which the multiple schemes of historical significance projected by the spectrum of political parties in Weimar Germany together constituted ripe opportunities for 'shifting the goalposts' with each successive government, as would be expected of a society that was given to time-discounting.[29] Lest one think that this phenomenon is confined to weak democracies struggling through volatile times, it is worth recalling how often such 'strong' and 'stable' democratic regimes as the USA and the UK have altered the definition of such basic indicators of welfare as 'unemployment' and 'inflation' in ways that have made political expediency seem to coincide with some sense of increased technical sophistication. Rawls notwithstanding, this is discounting raised to the level of statecraft.

However, it would be a mistake to regard this tendency as confined to politics. If anything, the modes of time discounting in science are *more* pronounced. A good way to understand these modes is in contrast to the sense of history championed in recent years by Fernand Braudel and Immanuel Wallerstein.[30] Here history is defined as the superimposition of temporal perspectives of varying durations, ranging from the point-like events that characterize moments in political history, through the periodic rhythms of business cycles, to the more enduring features of the natural environment that provide the background conditions for a people's long-term survival. These perspectives are distinguished primarily in terms of the extent to which past conditions continue largely unabated into the future. In contrast, the temporal perspectives enumerated below, while equally seen as superimposed, are based on the extent to which future conditions can reconstitute those in the past. In other words, the presence of time-discounting reflects the capacity for *reflexive historical awareness*.

To see exactly what I mean, consider the following three senses in which the future can reconstitute the past, which together represent an increasingly reflexive sense of historical awareness. I shall then illustrate these with familiar contemporary orientations to the history of science.

1 *What you do now changes what you can do later but not what you wanted.* This includes (at the individual level) self-defeating wants and (at the collective level) so-called 'counterfinality effects', the most notorious of which is perhaps Garrett Hardin's 'tragedy of the commons', whereby the individually rational actions of farmers eventuate in a collectively disastrous consequence, the depletion of grazing land. This perspective, used to justify arguments for environmental protection, presupposes that neither the past nor the future can be changed; rather, past wants remain constant and are simply thwarted in the future.

2 *What you do now changes what you will want.* This includes what social psychologists call 'adaptive preference formations', whereby one learns to like an outcome only once it has occurred, as in the complementary phenomena of sour grapes and sweet lemons noted earlier. Here future wants are reconstituted in the name of 'learning from experience', which is little more than an epistemological way of saying that past wants remain the same but future ones change.

3 *What you do now changes what you will have wanted.* Here history is rewritten in the comprehensive fashion depicted by George Orwell in *Nineteen Eighty-four* (1949), such that one no longer notices that a change has occurred. In other words, past wants are reconstituted to make it seem as though the future naturally continues the attempt to satisfy them. Any evidence of disruption is removed from the historical record, and hence the West's much vaunted sense of 'fearlessness' is manufactured.

Now for the corresponding examples from the history of science:

1 *The historian's perspective.* A good example is Kuhn's account of scientific puzzle-solving as eventuating in anomalies, the accumulation of which then precipitates a crisis in the paradigm. From this standpoint, a scientific revolution is always a long-term unintended consequence of the pursuit of normal science, not something that comes about by design. 'Rationality' in this context means nothing more grandiose than the research strategies that have proven most immediately useful to the scientific community, regardless of their long-term prospects.

2 *The philosopher's perspective.* Here history appears as a collective learning process, in which scientists are presented as regularly having to choose from among two or more theories. Thus, they must explicitly decide whether or not to continue their current research trajectory on the basis of its 'track record'. One thing that typically becomes evident from this track record is that long-standing conceptual problems with one's research programme can be offset as being of 'merely philosophical' interest, once enough empirical success has been registered.[31]

3 *The scientist's perspective.* The 'positivist' textbook history of science that is reconstituted with each paradigm-shift. It makes a science's current problem-set seem to be the one towards which all prior research had been implicitly heading. Even apparent diversions and errors are cast as being guided by an 'invisible hand' or 'cunning of reason', the full sense of which is typically realized by today's scientists, after having eluded their precursors.

Taken in succession, these three temporal perspectives can be read as constituting a 'slippery slope' of ever increasing rationalization for whatever happens. Each stage is a bit more reflexive in that the future is discounted a bit more heavily in anticipation that such a rationalization will occur. The Western philosopher of science who has been most critical of this slippery slope is Feyerabend, who became notorious for proposing a 'methodology' expressly designed to reduce the prospect of scientists making only the most conservative revisions of their theories when faced with discrepant empirical results.[32] Such conservative manoeuvres, according to Feyerabend, would be tantamount to an adaptive preference formation, as the scientists would be wishfully presuming that the discrepancy they have discovered exhausts everything that is wrong with their theory – a rather improbable presumption, especially when made in the name of 'methodological conservatism', a principle that is most naturally taken to mean that the anomalous finding is only the *beginning* of one's epistemic problems and that consequently one should presume that more trouble lies ahead. Nevertheless, by minimizing the significance of such anomalies, a research programme can easily appear to be 'progressing' by ever finer increments that asymptomatically approach a comprehensive understanding of the domain to which its theories putatively refer. The Feyerabendian antidote is to render the same evidence base compatible with as many different theories as possible, the coexistence of which would serve to remind the scientific community that even its historically privileged theories may be ultimately shown to have been radically off-base. This counter-discounting strategy may be compared with the one that Rawls implements in order to justify the redistribution of income under the guise of welfare. Specifically, both aim to instill an openness to alternative futures by defying our inductivist instincts to act as if our current situation will continue unabated in the future.

The fruits of forgetfulness: the relative advantage of backwardness

The economic historian Alexander Gerschenkron (1904–76) coined the expression, the *relative advantage of backwardness*, to capture the idea that latecomers to the Industrial Revolution made economic progress comparable to their predecessors in less time, not because they copied the pioneers, but because they learned from earlier mistakes and, more importantly, were forced to improvise for institutions and practices they lacked.[33] Gerschenkron's thesis trades on the intuition that necessity is the mother of invention, and that one can never be too efficient for one's good. Nevertheless, thinking about the advantages of backwardness has heuristic value at both the local and global level. Locally, it is useful for envisaging ways in which a society's need to respond to a situation not of one's own design can end up driving the subsequent course of its history. Globally, latecomer societies determine what had been 'necessary' versus 'contingent' in a trailblazer's success, thereby dispelling superstitious historical beliefs in the need to repeat exactly the same steps in order to achieve the same results.

All of this has a special relevance to our concerns in this book because the institution most responsible for the rise of science in the West (the university) was born of backwardness in the local sense, while the role of non-Westerners in defining science has largely involved capitalizing on backwardness in the global sense.

For his part, Gerschenkron was clearly targeting the unsophisticated character of certain Marxist invocations to 'learn from history', especially Lenin's attempt to use the economic history of Western Europe as a blueprint for Russia. Nevertheless, Gerschenkron's insight can be joined fruitfully with that of the neo-Marxist György Lukacs (1885–1971), who argued that, in modern capitalist societies, the proletariat occupy the appropriate class standpoint from which a revolutionary consciousness can emerge. What Lukacs had in mind was that the working class is ideally positioned to sort out the materialist 'wheat' from the ideological 'chaff' of the capitalist social order, for, while the working class does not have a vested interest in reproducing that order, its collaboration is required for the order's maintenance. A good example of the wheat and chaff requiring formal separation is the so-called iron law of wages: the tendency of workers' wages to gravitate around the subsistence level. David Ricardo (1772–1823) had presented this as an immutable principle of political economy that served the interests of both capitalist (who could then reinvest the surplus value drawn from the workers' unpaid labour) and worker (who would always be motivated to return to work in each day). If the history of capitalism were to be written from the standpoint of the proletariat, it would quickly become evident that Ricardo's putative law of human nature is really an abstract expression of historically contingent power relations. We have, then, the first step towards removing the odious power relations and institutionalizing the genuine efficiencies afforded by the capitalist mode of production in a more equitable social order.

Besides specific 'laws' of capitalism, the very idea of capitalism can itself be regarded as resulting from the relative advantage of backwardness. Starting with Robert Merton's adaptation of Max Weber's *The Protestant Ethic and the Spirit of Capitalism* (1904), it has been commonly assumed that the link between the rise of modern science and capitalism lies in some direct connection between science and technology, with the latter interpreted as the primary mechanism of wealth creation.[34] However, the history of

Western science tells a different story. Until the late nineteenth century, virtually all economically relevant technological innovations had been introduced by people whose formal scientific training was patchy at best. This point is often obscured by the eagerness with which the academic scientists of the day sought to *explain* why these innovations worked as well as they did, once they had already been deemed successful at a practical level. Not only did such explanations provide still wider societal legitimation for the technologies in question (by being deemed reliable according to known scientific principles), but they also legitimated the academic scientists themselves, whose relevance to the liberal arts curriculum was still in question. The relationship between the invention of the steam engine in the eighteenth century and the rise of the science of thermodynamics in the nineteenth century is the most obvious case in point. However, to locate the real sense in which the fates of science and capitalism have been coupled, one would do better to study the *autonomization* of, respectively, education and the economy that marked the devolution of the Roman Empire and the inadequacy of its feudal replacements. The world-systems theorist, Wallerstein, has stressed this point with regard to the rise of capitalism, but it is only now beginning to be forcefully made with regard to the rise of science in the West.[35]

According to Wallerstein, the increasing inability of imperial bureaucracies to redistribute farming surpluses and the local inefficiencies of manorial agricultural production opened the door to the organized forms of piracy and forced exchanges that eventually metamorphosed into 'trade routes' and 'market towns'. This is the context in which the West's modern preoccupation with limitless growth should be understood: as a kind of insurance against risk. The insatiable desire to accumulate wealth and transact goods – sentiments that were deemed intemperate by the classical Greek philosophers – were born of the need to pre-empt an anticipated loss, be it the result of decadence from within, barbarism from without or simply the Biblical decline of 'man'. Whereas Aristotle genuinely believed in the prospect of a steady-state economy in which people grew, made, bought, and sold only that which was necessary for their subsistence, during the Middle Ages this image was increasingly replaced with one in which economic well-being was bound to deteriorate if not actively maintained, and, perhaps, if not overcompensated.[36] From this need to concentrate so intently on the maintenance of economic well-being came capitalism.

Islam, the first topic of our next chapter, provides a striking contrast. Built as it was on arid land, Muslim civilization was held together by state-supported irrigation projects, whose construction and maintenance required the coordination of vast networks of technical workers. Because advances in science were thus readily seen as advances in statecraft, a considerable investment was made in developing the *madrasas*, the first residential colleges. However, the fates of these colleges were tied to the fortunes of their political patrons. Islamic law did not guarantee the colleges the corporate autonomy that would enable their inquiries to continue in perpetuity. That idea – the *university* – was a Western innovation, one born of the disorganization of feudal Europe, where rulers were often more than happy to grant autonomy to self-constituting groups that kept the peace and abided by minimal standards of political loyalty.[37] It was still a long way from establishing institutions of pure inquiry to legitimating the natural sciences as we know them today. However, a decisive point was that under Roman law, the category of *universitas* covered not only (or even primarily) institutions of higher learning, but also craft and trade guilds. While this equality of legal status enabled a kind of commerce between 'scholars' and 'artisans' in the cities that never really existed in the more highly stratified civilizations of the East, the sight of the different classes jostling for space in overcrowded streets was bemoaned at the time as symptomatic of social disorder.[38] Indeed, if most intellectuals of the High Middle Ages had their way, they would have preferred the strict separation of 'head' and 'hands' that characterized classical Athens and Rome. In other words, what are now widely regarded to have been the social and economic preconditions for the rise of science in Europe were regarded in their day as signs of *decline*.

Notes

1 Wolpert (1992). The reference is to the first Greek natural philosopher, Thales of Miletus (624–546 BC), who claimed that water is the universal principle.

2 The social epistemology of this late turn-of-the-century historical sensibility is explored in Fuller (1994d, e).

3 Needham (1969).
4 Fuller (1993b: 210–13).
5 Sivin (1982).
6 Cohen (1994: 479).
7 Shapin and Schaffer (1985).
8 Fukuyama (1992).
9 Winner (1977).
10 Weatherford (1988).
11 A good discussion of both movements' relevance to science can be found in Harding (1991).
12 Keller (1985).
13 Diop (1991).
14 Bernal (1987).
15 Van Sertima (1986).
16 Leplin (1984).
17 McGuire and Rattansi (1966)
18 Gellner (1988).
19 Adams (1971: 555ff.).
20 Ainslie (1992).
21 Price (1993).
22 Rawls (1971).
23 Parfit (1984).
24 Elster (1984).
25 Aron (1957: 150).
26 Febvre and Martin (1971).
27 Eisenstein (1979).
28 Butterfield (1955: 79).
29 Mannheim (1936).
30 Wallerstein (1991: 185–226).
31 Laudan (1977).
32 Feyerabend (1975).
33 Gerschenkron (1962).
34 Merton (1970).
35 Wallerstein (1991: 125–48); see also Huff (1993).
36 Arndt (1978).
37 Dorn (1991: 110–21).
38 LeGoff (1993).

6

Western Science from the Outside In: The View from Islam and Japan

Islam: scientific autonomy as Western sacrilege

Islam presents an interesting challenge to both under- and over-determinationist metahistories of science. However, the challenge is easily lost amidst the blizzard of discourse surrounding *multiculturalism*, which, at least in its Western incarnations, tends to homogenize the sense of 'difference' that non-Western cultures supposedly provide to the West. Take a canonical multiculturalist work, such as Edward Said's *Orientalism* (1978), which dwells on the portrayal of Asiatic peoples in European literature and scholarship over the past 200 years.[1] By treating the exoticization of Asia as itself a uniform phenomenon ripe for deconstruction, Said unwittingly continues the tendency to homogenize difference. Of course, after Said's work, the exoticism has gone into reverse. The phenomenon of Orientalism is now taken to reveal more about how Europeans think than about how Asians think – but the lumping of 'them' versus 'us' remains.[2]

A casualty of this approach is that Westerners rarely appreciate the difference between a culture whose roots are virtually independent of Europe's and a culture that is largely an alternative development of the common heritage it shares with modern Europe. In terms of Asia, China epitomizes the former, and Islam the latter.[3] Here it is instructive to examine a group of cosmopolitan Muslim intellectuals collectively known as the 'Islamic revivalists', for whom Islam's unique historical status posed a specific practical challenge: Ahmad Khan (1817–98), Jamaluddin Afghani (1839–97), and Mohammed Abduh (1849–1905).[4] Writing in the late nineteenth century, they upheld Islam as the revealed word of Allah, but admitted that the Muslim world had fallen into decline, due largely to the spiritual failure of its own leaders, which made it vulnerable to the West's opportunism.

However, the Islamic revivalists found themselves in an awkward position with regard to Muslim history. On the one hand, they wanted to claim for Islam many of the achievements, especially in science, that the West took be definitive of its own sense of progress; on the other, while conceding backwardness, they still wanted to distance any future development of Islamic science from the more patently materialistic and destructive features of Western science. Thus, we may think of these reformers as having agreed on the following five theses.

1 Islam and Christianity have essentially the same origin and represent alternative ways of continuing that common heritage.
2 Initially, Muslims deliberately refused to follow the West's path of allowing science to become so autonomous from the rest of society that it frequently threatened its moral constitution. In contrast, the West has pursued knowledge at the expense of wisdom.
3 Nevertheless, Islam's own historical trajectory must equally be rejected, as it has led to an ossified doctrinal consensus that has failed to accommodate changes that have taken place in the world over the past five centuries.
4 But the revival of Islam must do more than project a utopia that ignores the Muslim world's long period of decline. Rather, it must learn from that history and selectively appropriate elements of Western history that could aid in Islam's revival.
5 The rhetorical challenge of modern Islam, then, is to return to that original fork on the road where Christianity and Islam parted company and to pursue a form of knowledge infused with the teaching of the Qur'an that is at the same time recognizable as scientifically progressive.

Looking over this list, the extent to which the mutual understanding of Islam and the West, until very recently, has rested on common historical misunderstandings is striking. Two sorts of misunderstanding are especially apparent from the onset of Islamic revivalism. The first is the failure to see that the social conditions for promoting science in Islam and the West were still not so far apart, even perhaps as late as the time the revivalists were writing. The second is the failure to see that the West has indirectly benefited from its having been politically, economically and culturally less advanced than Asia for most of its history.[5]

Let us start with a question. In what sense had the West surpassed Islam in science in 1900? I mean to signal an issue raised earlier, when discussing the relative strengths and weaknesses of the two metahistories of science – namely, that to explain the origin of a concept or technique is not to explain its diffusion. On the one hand, several philosophically inspired distinctions threaten to turn this observation into a banality. Logicians routinely invoke the 'genetic fallacy' to ward off those who would judge the validity of an argument on the basis of its origins. After Whewell, philosophers of science have routinely distinguished contexts of 'discovery' and 'justification' to similar effect. On the other hand, even relatively sophisticated historical accounts of science, such as Thomas Kuhn's, continue to focus their narratives entirely on front-line researchers (as opposed to those who apply or teach the knowledge), who are themselves presented as completing the vision set out by some heroic predecessor, as in the case of the 200-year 'Newtonian paradigm' in physics. At the start of Chapter 5, I noted that scientists are especially prone to see things in Kuhn's way. To counteract this bias towards the heroic, it is worth remembering that the Scientific Revolution did not occur overnight *even in the West*. There are some very substantial timelags between the emergence and adoption of revolutionary scientific ideas. A good example is the modern science of anatomy and physiology, one of the great Renaissance accomplishments of Andreas Vesalius (1514–64) and his Italian colleagues, which did not figure in Western medical practice for another three centuries.[6] In other words, explaining the spread of science across the face of Europe itself turns out to be just as much a matter of 'uneven development' as explaining its spread across the rest of the world.

The Islamic revivalists thought they could explain why science (supposedly) spread so much more quickly in the West than across Islam. They were in general agreement that Islam's failure to adopt

the Western practice of separating Church and State was the source
of the natural sciences' failure to gain a proper footing in the major
Muslim universities, be it the Aligarh near Delhi (Khan), the University of Istanbul (Afghani), or the El-Azhar in Cairo (Abduh).
What the reformers had in mind, of course, was not the removal of
religious training from the curriculum, but rather the elimination of
theological oversight on scientific subjects. Yet, while Western
observers encouraged these reforms, it was not because their own
institutions of higher education were fully in the hands of secular
authorities, or even that the elimination of theological oversight
had demonstrably improved Western institutions. Indeed, the
country where the laity's victory over the clerics was most loudly
advertised – France under the Third Republic – was also the one
whose institutions of higher learning were in most disrepute, mainly
because 'secularization' had opened the door to faculty blurring criteria of intellectual distinction and public notoriety, a tendency that
arguably continues to the present day.[7]

Moreover, one should not conclude from the fact that ecclesias-
tical authorities were not directly involved in the governance of
European nation-states that they had lost all control over the reins
of power in the West. Even in the scientifically most advanced
country of the time, Germany, the number of university students
matriculating in all the natural sciences combined did not equal the
number in theology until 1898.[8] Even more striking is the case of
Germany's world-famous interdisciplinary research institutes, the
Kaiser Wilhelm Gesellschaften (now called the Max Planck Institutes), which pooled the resources of the academy, the state, and
industry to develop the first of what are now regarded as 'Big
Science' projects. The force behind their development was the
country's leading theologian, Adolf von Harnack (1851–1930), in
his role as research minister.[9] A secret of the West's ongoing
success, then, was not the marginalization of Christian theology, but
its active support of the natural sciences. Lest we forget, Whewell,
the man who coined 'scientist' in English as the name of a profession (training for which deserved a place in the Oxbridge curriculum) was himself a confirmed Anglican priest.

Over the past century, it has also been common to bemoan the fact
that, in the Muslim countries, the diffusion of scientific and technical innovations was largely restricted to the military institutes and
not integrated into the general university curriculum. In particular,

the decline of the Ottoman Empire has been attributed to such a blockage in the transmission of scientific ideas.[10] However, this pattern is not so very different from the West's own experience. In Britain, France, Germany, and the USA, the first institutions of higher education to make natural science and technology a part of their ordinary curriculum were likewise the military academies, which had begun to evolve into full-fledged polytechnics by the end of the eighteenth century, as ambitious rulers followed Napoleon's lead in regarding civil engineering projects as a productive way to deploy their professional soldiers in peacetime. In any case, this was over a century after the Scientific Revolution had taken place and nearly a full century before these technical subjects were generally seen as fit for genteel civilian consumption.[11] How long, then, did it take for science to spread across the West itself?

The answer varies from country to country, of course, but it generally corresponds to the introduction of compulsory mass education towards the end of the nineteenth century and the insinuation of scientific studies, often quite basic, in vocational training at roughly the same time. Indeed, the most significant difference between the educational patterns in European and Muslim countries was to be found not in the tertiary sector – where the Muslim figures were often more impressive than the European ones – but at the primary and secondary school level, where the Europeans were much more effective at what we would now describe as 'laying down the infrastructure for an information society' by ensuring basic levels of literacy and numeracy. Thus, 100 years ago, Egypt's El-Azhar enrolled over 10,000 students in a country with a population of 5.5 million, whereas the combined enrolment of *all* British universities in the same period was 20,000 students from a population of 39 million.[12] The university curriculum in both countries was highly biased towards theological and humanistic studies, and the academic elite were generally suspicious of scientific and technical subjects. However, upon examining educational differences below the elite level, it immediately becomes clear why Britain was the resident colonial power in Egypt, and not the other way around. Specifically, the basic literacy rate of Britain was ten times that of Egypt.[13] Unfortunately, because the history of science is still conceptualized – in both East and West – as the circulation of elites, the overriding significance of a policy as humble as the provision of basic technical training for the masses can easily be neglected.

So far, I have spoken about the Islamic revivalists as if they held identical views, when in fact they represent interestingly different approaches for the mutual accommodation of Islam and the Western scientific world-view. A chronological ordering of their activities reveals an increasingly critical engagement with the content of Western science.

The first revivalist, Ahmad Khan, was eventually knighted by Queen Victoria for his work in promoting cross-cultural understanding among the Muslims, Hindus, and Christians of India. Khan sought common intellectual ground among the three world religions. This led him to endorse a form of naturalism based on the metaphysics of atomism, which resonated with the Greek roots common to Christianity and Islam, as well as the current scientific age. In addition, atomism's belief in bodily death as a transition in the recombination of atoms was reminiscent of the Hindu doctrine of the transmigration of souls. However, Khan was criticized by more radical Muslims for stressing precisely those features of the Oriental heritage that were most conducive to rendering them submissive in the face of Western imperialism. After all, the ethic classically associated with atomism had been the passive acceptance of the ephemeral nature of material forms, which in practice led to fatalism, since the principles of atomic combination were taken to be permanently below the threshhold of human perception. Indeed, atomistic thinking first became widespread among the Greeks, as the doctrine of Epicurus, only once Alexander the Great had conquered them. It is true that by the end of the nineteenth century, atomism had become the ascendant philosophy among Western experimental scientists, who used it to argue that there is a limit to reality – the atomic constituents of matter that is the ultimate goal of physical inquiry. However, such a philosophy only helped those who already held power as it seemed to implicitly downgrade the observable world in which the bulk of humanity dwelled. Indeed, this argument figured not only in the Muslim debates but also in Western ones at roughly the same time, especially Ernst Mach's 'last stand' against atomism as the vehicle of elitist science more generally.

Much more politically assertive was Jamaluddin Afghani, an inspiring and controversial speaker in radical forums throughout Asia, Africa and Europe. Afghani operated with a bifurcated strategy for elite and mass audiences. He urged the elites to concede the

West's indictment of Islam's decadence as mostly self-inflicted, as religious leaders exerted so much control over civil affairs that they stunted the growth of Muslim science after its medieval heyday. Indeed, when addressing European audiences, Afghani seemed to suggest that all religions, Islam included, were ultimately symbolic expressions of group solidarity that, over time, would be replaced by the rational forms of authority that characterized modern Western science and government. Afghani was clearly impressed by the great strides that Germany had made towards political unification, which enabled it to challenge Britain's position as the leading imperial power by the end of the nineteenth century. Thus, he had no illusion that the acceptance of science was tantamount to an endorsement of the military–industrial complex that continued to be regarded as barbarous by many traditional Muslim intellectuals. However, Afghani also believed that the secret to science's strength would be, at least in the short term, unavailable to the bulk of the Muslim peoples, who were better presented with the usual demonic image of the West that required a reassertion of their commitment to the faith. Not surprisingly, both the elite and mass messages ran afoul of Islam's religious authorities, and Afghani found himself a political fugitive for most of his life.

Nevertheless, Afghani's strategy was deeply rooted in the history of Islam itself, especially the Double Truth doctrine of the great twelth- century Spanish Muslim philosopher alternatively known as Ibn-Rushd or Averroës (1126–98), who must be counted as one of the most interesting figures in the history of cross-cultural reception. After concluding our survey of Islamic revivalist attitudes towards science, we shall delve a bit more deeply into the Averroist sensibility, as much of the subsequent intellectual development of Christendom and Islam – why the one embraced the trajectory that led to modern science and the other rejected it – can be explained by the striking difference in how Averroës was received.

For his part, Muhammad Abduh, the spiritual leader of Cairo, was keen to contain the potentially corrosive effects of Afghani's Averroism. While Abduh conceded the decadence of Islam, he refused to grant Afghani that it was self-inflicted, but held that it was the direct result of its Western captors who instilled the sense of fatalism that the likes of Khan wished to rationalize. Moreover, had Islam been permitted to run its natural course, it would have reaped science's generally acknowledged benefits without the destructive consequences that have accompanied them. Abduh's reasoning was based on Islam's greater insistence than Christianity that knowledge production be in service of a communal ethic, one that would have never permitted the sort of runaway technology which Westerners misidentified as 'science for its own sake'. As Abduh saw it, most forms of Christianity remained focused on the hereafter, and hence refused to take a more active interest (other than occasional censorship) in shaping the scientific world-view that had indiscriminately come to underwrite both beneficial and destructive technologies.

What is nowadays known as 'Islamic fundamentalism' embodies many of Abduh's attitudes, tinged, however, with Afghani's *realpolitik* attitude towards the power of science and often the rejection of local Muslim authorities, who are regarded as having given too much ground to secular powers. Thus, recent years have witnessed an unprecedented number of Muslims matriculating in the natural sciences and engineering at Western universities, all the while upholding the belief that the knowledge they acquire remains in captivity until harnessed to the unifying vision of Islam. The figure who has most embodied this unique combination of Islamic religious renewal with a strategic embrace of Western science has been Abduh's fellow Egyptian, Sayyid Qutb (1906–66).[14]

The phenomenon of Islamic revivalism raises three general issues about the nature of science that would not have come out so clearly, had we focused exclusively on the history of Western science. In the first place, there is something strange, or at least idiosyncratic, about the Western idea of pursuing knowledge for its own sake without any specification of the sort of knowledge that is worth having. From a philosophical standpoint, Islamic revivalism questions the sharp line that Westerners have drawn between *epistemology* and *ethics*, that is, the pursuit of inquiry from the pursuit of the good.[15] However, the presence of this division in the Western science curriculum – a source of science's so-called value-neutral character – has enabled devout Muslims to become competent scientists without having to renounce their faith and become 'Westernized' in the process. Instead, they simply insert their own values where the West provides no moral direction. Islam's difficulties with the West's singleminded embrace of science is instructive in a second sense. The many ends that human beings are expected to pursue simultaneously in one lifetime make it unreasonable to demand that knowledge be pursued for its own sake – that is, as efficiently as possible, regardless of its impact on other aspects of one's life, not to mention the lives of others. Thirdly, as the vexed legacy of Averroës will shortly reveal, we may ask how the pursuit of knowledge can be regarded as a universal human good, if, as Averroës thought, the mass of humanity had to be sheltered from science's potentially destabilizing consequences? Contrary to what even the Islamic revivalists themselves thought, the West's answer to this question came in the form of a short-term incapacity that provided the basis for a long-term virtue, the 'relative advantage of backwardness', in Gerschenkron's terms.

From the mid-eighth century to the mid-seventeeth century, the Muslim realm was more far-flung, tight-knit, and wealthy than the feudal kingdoms and city-states scattered across the face of Christendom. Indeed, a commonplace among medieval historians is that 'Europe' would never have been such an attractive idea to rally around, had the continent's inhabitants not shared the threat of an expanding Islam. In the words of the great medieval historian, Henri Pirenne (1862–1935), 'No Charlemagne without Muhammad'. A more controversial, but probably no less true, claim is that the Mediterranean regions of Europe most often cast as innovators in science and technology during the Renaissance were acting more in the 'Japanese' spirit of reverse engineering with the intent of producing technically improved versions of Muslim (and, for that matter, Chinese) innovations. However, the interconnectedness of Muslim rule, which enabled relatively good patterns of communication among scholars in Spain, Egypt, and Persia, also made it easier to subject intellectual life to direct political control. In some cases, this had a clearly salutary effect. Consider the famed Muslim drive for synthesis, which made Arabic the first genuinely cosmopolitan language of thought, one that integrated the heritages of Graeco–Roman, Judaeo–Christian, and Indo–Iranian cultures under a single conceptual rubric long before Latin came to play that role. That drive was nurtured by the pedagogical needs of students training for civil service. The downside of political control became apparent once religious and secular authority was synchronized to such an extent that the Muslim world became a *de facto* theocracy. This did not come about very quickly or by design, but nevertheless was the result of taking seriously the idea that a common faith was the ultimate source of legitimation for so many people encompassed under one regime.

Although Islam's sense of the sacred, like Christianity's, is located in the believer's encounter with the Word of God as transcribed in His Holy Book, professional interpreters of God's Word, the *ulama*, soon emerged. While this development bears some resemblance to the priestly class of the Roman Catholic Church, there were two important differences. First, Christendom never enjoyed the degree of political integration needed for the enforcement of a religious orthodoxy, however much St Augustine would have wished to establish a 'City of God' on Earth. Heretical religious leaders inspired by a bewildering array of imaginative readings of the Bible can be found throughout the history of Christianity. In most cases the Church was powerless to do more than threaten them. Moreover, as the Church's own material stakes grew, it was forced to depend on the goodwill of secular leaders for protection. Thus, Christ's dictum, 'Render unto Caesar what is Caesar's', but render unto God what is God's' eventually became a slogan of mutual accommodation. Institutions developed – notably the confessional – that made it relatively easy for kings and princes to be absolved from the morally dubious aspects of their lives. A second difference, one resulting from the Church's accommodation of the religious and the secular, was that the preservation of Christian doctrine became increasingly identified with monastic and scholastic specialists who resided in abbeys and universities out of the line of political fire. By contrast, the Muslim *ulama* held increasingly influential secular positions alongside their religious functions that enabled them to mediate, survive and even flourish in the midst of dynastic infighting. The most important historical consequence of this difference is that Christendom was more tolerant than Islam of the Platonic idea that there are two truths, one for an elite sheltered from political interference and one for the masses.

Medieval Europe owed most of its understanding of Greek philosophy – and certainly the revival of interest in Aristotle and natural philosophy – to Averroës and other Muslim commentators. Yet, the Muslims themselves have often been characterized as 'anti-philosophical' in outlook. At work here is a difference in the social function of religion and philosophy in the two cultures, where 'philosophy' is a non-theological science, the pursuit of knowledge for its own sake, regardless of where it may lead. Averroës is primarily known to Muslims as the person who mounted the last great defence of philosophy against the religious proscriptions of

Al-Ghazali (1058–1111). Al-Ghazali, the leading theologian of his day, had argued that according to the Qur'an, God is capable of directly intervening in worldly affairs. Moreover, it is this capacity that enables God to be the sort of being who can command the respect of humans. Any philosophy that does not proceed from these premises, concluded Al-Ghazali, is simply 'incoherent'. If it appears that God can exist outside of space and time, yet continue to operate within it, then that mystery merely exemplifies the quantum leap from human to divine intelligence. Averroës, drawing on his own background as a jurist, replied that, as a matter of fact, the Qur'an offered conflicting accounts of God's capacities, which required higher-order interpretive resolution. Here auxiliary philosophical considerations could play a decisive role. In particular, God would not be a perfect being if he could be influenced by events in space and time (such as prayer). Indeed, that God would feel the need to monitor his Creation suggests that he had not done it right the first time. From this Averroës concluded that God must wholly transcend space and time, and therefore be literally uninvolved in the everyday affairs of his Creation.

This argument had two important but controversial consequences. One, which Averroës presented in the spirit of reconciliation with his theological opponents, was that philosophy could destroy the faith of weaker minds and thus could only be cultivated by a scholarly elite divorced from any religious functions. Presumably, in his unfettered search for truth, the philosopher would retain and even strengthen his faith, since it would be purified of unreliable analogies and images that appeal to the mass mind. This was a familiar theme from Plato's critique of rhetoric and his remarks about the training of philosophers. However, Plato's version of the Double Truth doctrine was proposed in the spirit of philosophers exercising self-restraint by not letting secular ambition pervert their intellectual powers. Averroës's arguments were made in a rather different context, one which aimed more simply to keep open a space for philosophical arguments to be aired. Read in these terms, Averroës seemed to insinuate that theologians like Al-Ghazali were basically in the business of manufacturing myths for popular consumption, while the 'real' truth-seekers deserved to be sheltered from such a corrupt practice. This clearly flew in the face of Islam's self-image as a world religion ever in search of converts to the Word of Allah. Though he claimed to be a devout Muslim,

Averroës's main concern, like Plato's, was that the pursuit of inquiry not be compromised by public interference. Thus, he wanted less to expand the spiritual horizons of the masses than to contain their worst effects.

The second consequence of Averroës's argument was only fully developed once Thomas Aquinas (1225–74) introduced his work to Christendom. If we grant that divine Creation is already in its completed and perfect form, as Averroës did, then a good way to discern the divine plan would seem to be by studying Creation itself, which is to say that natural philosophy becomes more than just a permissible activity alongside Biblical commentary. Indeed, taken to its logical extreme, Averroës could be interpreted as saying that even God is bound by the laws of nature, a claim that would bring him very close to the modern sensibility of regarding the search for regularities in nature as a surer route to God's mind than even Biblical commentary. Given these interpretations of his work, Averroës unsurprisingly earned the honour of having a Christian heresy named after him. But the religious condemnation heaped upon the 'Averroists' resident at the University of Paris by the local bishop in 1277 did little more than expel them from the university and divest them of their theological credentials. Thereafter, the leading Latin Averroist, Siger of Brabant (1235–84), fled to Northern Italy, where his followers spent the next three centuries training the people who would become the scientific leaders of the Renaissance, most notably Galileo.

Since the time of Al-Ghazali, Islam has generally held that the pursuit of science is justifiable only if it serves the needs of the Muslim community (which potentially includes all of humanity). In practice, this has meant that Muslim attitudes towards science have veered between two extremes, at least if we take the history of Western science as the norm. On the one hand, there has been great hostility towards any new knowledge that might cast aspersions on the validity of the Qur'an. On the other, there has been great enthusiasm for organizing all forms of knowledge under the value system licensed in the Qur'an. In contrast to these extremes, and reflecting at least as much political feasibility as intellectual tolerance, Christianity has typically settled for permitting the pursuit of science to the extent that it did not openly contradict the Bible or the Church Fathers. Galileo managed to aggravate his Jesuit inquisitors because he refused to accept the compatibility of

Copernicus's sun-centred universe and the Bible. He held that the two contradicted each other and that Copernicus was right.

In the Western tradition, William of Ockham provides an interesting point of comparison with Al-Ghazali in terms of their attitudes towards the relationship between God and his Creation. Ockham is nowadays known primarily for 'Ockham's Razor', his injunction not to postulate the existence of entities unless they are needed to explain the phenomenon at hand. In today's world, Ockham's Razor is the principle most likely to be invoked when, say, evolutionary biologists want to show that it is not necessary to invoke a divine plan to explain the origin and development of life on Earth. However, in terms of our previous discussion, Ockham is noteworthy for having been one of the scholastics whose Parisian teachings conformed to the 1277 edict. Both Al-Ghazali and Ockham agreed that God can create any possible world he wants and that we have no way of knowing whether the one before our eyes is the ultimately real one. Nevertheless, the different social positions of the two theologians conditioned the conclusions they drew from this set of shared beliefs. Al-Ghazali, who ministered to the faithful, stressed the idea that one should be grateful to Allah that the world displays any order whatsoever, with the precise identity of that order forever remaining a mystery. Ockham, who taught only those enrolled in university studies, used the unfathomability of God's mind as an opportunity to entertain alternative hypotheses about the nature of physical reality, including supposing that – contrary to common sense – the Earth moved relative to the sun, rather than vice versa. Not surprisingly, the expulsion of the Averroists from the theology faculty, combined with the remaining theologians' freedom to explore divine possibilities esoterically, led Pierre Duhem to argue that the foundations of the modern scientific mindset were laid down by the 1277 condemnation.[16]

Moreover, the explicitly communal character of Islam meant that anything that smacked of an elitist appeal would have been seen as divisive to Muslim authorities, whereas elitism could always be justified in the Christian context as an effort to set an example of enlightened spirituality for the rest of the community to follow. In this way, the Platonic desire for a static hierarchy of believers, each equipped with a competence appropriate to their station, metamorphosed in Christendom into a dynamic programme, an inchoate theory of *progress* that laid down the steps through which one needed to pass to acquire the superior knowledge already possessed by the vanguard. Given that Averroës justified his support of an elite philosophical class on the basis of internal contradictions present in the Qur'an, it is perhaps not surprising that his proposal was seen as insulting the intelligence of those who ministered to the faithful. Moreover, the fact that Averroës's arguments were cast in the elite language of philosophy ensured that the Christian scholastics would be more likely to pick up on them than rank and file Muslims.

The rhetorical strategy of his Christian descendant, Galileo, could not be more different. First, he justified the examination of arguments that went beyond Scripture on the grounds that the Church fathers had not the opportunity in their day to examine the evidence (say, through the telescope) that became available only in Galileo's time. In other words, Galileo was careful not to imply that the failure of Scripture was related to some intellectual short-coming – such as inconsistency – on the part of its author and interpreters; rather, the failure was diagnosed in terms of the simple fact that they were not acquainted with techniques of knowing that had become available only after the time they lived. Admittedly, Galileo's self-defence was not entirely successful as he was under house arrest for the final years of his life. However, his writings were themselves sufficiently accessible, with many written in the Italian vernacular, to enable a relatively large portion of the literate population to consider and extend his initiatives, which culminated in what we now regard as the Scientific Revolution that transpired later in the seventeenth century.

When Afghani sought a Western model for breathing new life into Muslim civilization, he turned to the great Protestant reformer Martin Luther (1483–1546), whose promise of spiritual rebirth was a response to the Church's morally uneven influence on the world.[17] Moreover, the regimes proposed by such reformers as Luther and John Calvin (1509–64) resembled what had already existed in the Muslim world for the past 250 years: activities were permitted only if they could be suffused with religious significance. Thus, while the Lutheran university in Wittenberg, Germany was the first academic institution to teach Copernican astronomy, the faculty carefully stripped the theory of its revolutionary explanatory framework and treated it as a refinement of Ptolemy's celestial readings. In this way, they avoided Luther's own legendary suspicions that Copernicanism was a papist plot for adding yet another layer of mediating authority between the faithful and their understanding of Scripture, let alone common sense. For its part, Calvin's Geneva, the closest that Protestantism ever got to a pure theocracy, countenanced a variety of science policy initiatives that included the execution of competing reformers such as Michael Servetus (1511–53), whose account of the lungs' contribution to the blood's circulation appeared in a theological tract that denied the Holy Trinity and the need for infant baptism. However, in the case of Copernicus, Calvin seemed to reinvent the Double Truth stance, when he criticized the astronomer's followers more for inflaming the masses with thoughts they could not handle than with the pursuit of novel astronomical hypotheses as such.[18] In light of this lingering Averroism, it may be reasonable to interpret the frequent calls by natural scientists in seventeenth-century Europe to have their activities sheltered from religious or public scrutiny as a subtle strategy for maintaining order in the larger polity. In contrast, the Roman Catholic Church issued a characteristically divided judgement on the work of that Polish cathedral canon, Nicolaus Copernicus (1473–1543): while the Jesuits were persecuting Galileo for Copernicanism in Rome, they were also promulgating Copernican doctrine as part of their missionary work in China. The Protestant sects that failed to establish political sovereignty tended to be still more liberal about the new scientific ideas, most notably in Britain and France, which housed the first scientific societies of any considerable duration and support.

The point of this inventory of religious attitudes towards science is not to credit or blame certain religions, but rather to highlight the indirect epistemic advantage afforded by the political incapacity to impose a doctrinal consensus.[19] As a point of statecraft, this insight is normally credited to the main philosophical architect of the US Constitution, James Madison (1751–1836). Under the rubric of 'checks and balances', Madison commended the incapacity to impose a doctrinal consensus as a design feature of good government. Similarly, religions will appear scientifically progressive when they can use science to challenge an orthodoxy that threatens the expression of their basic beliefs, but *not* when they can enforce a common mind-set on their members. For example, if (or rather, *when*, given the fallibility of even the most indomitable of scientific theories) the theory of biological evolution by natural selection yields to a version of evolution that incorporates a sense of cosmic intelligence, it is certain that some historians will portray

	Islam	*The West*
Metatheory of knowledge	Ethics (knowledge is a means to other ends)	Epistemology (knowledge is an end in itself)
Politics of science	Science is good in so far as it benefits society	Society is good in so far as it advances science
The Double Truth doctrine	Not tolerated by design	Tolerated by default
The fate of science	Arrested by an elite	Diffused to the masses

Figure 6.1   The relationships between science and religion in Islam and the West.

Creationists as having been prescient for highlighting the sort of anomalous evidence that today they brandish at evolutionists to little avail. Arguments that now appear reactionary will probably contribute to the next scientific revolution as 'the return of the repressed', in Freudian terms. If so, then much of the moralistic passion that Westerners find disturbing about Islamic science will appear in a positive light once Western science is repatriated to an ethically unified world-view.

The rather paradoxical historical relationships between science and religion in Islam and the West are summarized in Figure 6.1.

Japan: scientific autonomy as Western superstition

When people talk about the 'Japanese miracle' nowadays, they usually mean the country's rapid ascendency after the Second World War, understood in terms of its remarkably productive corporate culture. However, Japan has been generally recognized as one of the five or six leading world powers since the first decade of the twentieth century. This was less than half a century after it had officially opened its doors to Western influences, following over two centuries of self-imposed isolation, in large measure a reaction to overzealous missionary work by the Jesuits. The real 'Japanese miracle', then, occurred in the 35 years between 1869 and 1904, as the country moved from a declining feudal order, through national consolidation, and finally to an imperial world power. During this period, Japan accomplished each year what had taken at least ten years for Europe to achieve. For our purposes, the crucial transition starts with the selective appropriation of Western science and technology and culminates in the first military defeat of a Western power (Russia) by a non-Western power (Japan) on the basis of superior technical skill and new machine-gun technology. However, the conclusion of the 1905 Russo–Japanese War had farther reaching consequences than simply marking the emergence of a new superpower. More importantly, it demonstrated that Western science and technology could be successfully transferred to a country that had not first been Westernized.

All of this came as shocking news to Westerners, whose theories of progress and modernization presupposed that material and intellectual development required that one pass through a more or less fixed sequence of stages, which together constituted the logic underlying European history. Although one immediately thinks of the great nineteenth-century philosophers of history, Hegel, Marx, Comte, and Spencer, this idea is still very much alive today, especially in an economic context, as in Francis Fukuyama's hotly debated 'end of history' thesis. At a subtler level, the idea has informed Piagetian developmental psychology, according to which 2000 years of the history of Western physics are recapitulated in the first dozen years of childhood. Even the influential theory of scientific change put forward by Kuhn admits of a Piagetian pedigree in its treatment of the history of physics from 1620 to 1920 as a template for all properly functioning knowledge systems.[20] In each of these cases, the European historical record is treated, not as a contingently related series of events, but as evidence for a repeatable – perhaps even universalizable – pattern of directed growth. In terms of the two metahistories outlined in Chapter 5, we have here an unholy alliance of under- and overdeterminationism, whereby history is converted into the following logic: 'Perhaps the Scientific Revolution need not have happened, but once it did, its diffusion became inevitable'. At that point, *universalism* becomes synonymous with *eurocentrism* and quite opposed to something that could be genuinely called *globalism*.

It would be difficult to overestimate the grip that this precise sense of eurocentrism has had on the global imagination over the past 300 years. Russia is perhaps the country that has been most under the eurocentric spell. Peter the Great (1672–1725) and Lenin (1870–1924) represent two forms of captivation, one more exogenous and the other more endogenous. When Peter the Great set out to modernize Russia, he did not merely import books and artifacts from Western Europe. Armed with tax incentives, he managed to lure the Enlightenment luminaries who wrote the books and designed the artifacts so that they could continue their activities in his country, presumably spreading their interests and competences to the natives. For his part, Lenin centralized the economy and consolidated class consciousness to speed up a process that he thought was already occurring in his country (and would eventually occur in every country), namely, the transition from feudalism to capitalism and finally socialism. All the more poignant, then, that Russia should have been the victim of Japan's 1905 existential refutation of eurocentrism. Just based on the West's own history, the Japanese link between military victory and scientific achievement should not have come as such a surprise. After all, the first inklings that Europe was gaining 'world-historic' ground on Islam was when the Ottoman Turks were held off from taking Vienna in 1683. This was one of the first skirmishes in which a 'scientific' understanding of ballistics revealed its practical benefits.[21] Over the next century, Western observers gradually reinterpreted the distinctive features of Muslim culture as marks of decadence rather than sublimity.

The opening up of Japan to the West is traditionally said to have begun in 1853, when Commodore Matthew Perry parked a quarter of the US Navy in Tokyo harbour until the Japanese agreed to sign a highly imbalanced trade treaty. However, Japan's programme of 'defensive modernization' began in earnest only with the restoration of the Meiji Emperor Mutsuhito in 1869.[22] At that point, Japan was already one of the world's most populous and urbanized countries (Tokyo had already been the world's largest city for a century). The feudal order of *samurai* had long ago traded in their military skills for managerial ones, converting a set of fiefdoms into an efficient network for the implementation of imperial reforms in education and industry.[23] The ease with which lingering Japanese feudalism was translated into the infrastructure of the world's fastest growing capitalist economy during the last quarter of the nineteenth century refuted some of the most distinctive and pervasive theories in Western sociology – at the time of their formulation! I refer here not only to the Marxist claim that feudal social relations must be disrupted to enable the rise of capitalism but also to the general view that the difference between 'traditional' and 'modern' social forms is clearly marked. In the case of science, we need look no further than to the recruitment of physicists and engineers from the ranks of the *samurai*, whose traditionally hierarchical and competitive cast of mind was effectively sublimated in the management of large research units focused on the rapid solution of well defined technical problems.[24]

The most striking feature of Japan's policy of defensive modernization was the management of foreign influence. In the first quarter century of modernization, Japanese students were sent overseas to study at European universities, while European and American educators were imported to advise on national educational and research policy. However, once Japan began its own campaign of imperial expansion, the foreigners were sent home, and the students were encouraged to spend less time abroad. The Japanese listened politely to the foreigners, but felt under no obligation to follow all of their advice. The Japanese were especially sensitive to the historically contingent pattern of science's institutionalization in the West. From this perspective, the migratory tendencies of German students, who rarely did all their courses at one university, suited the Japanese 'pick-and-choose' mentality better than the more campus-bound students at Oxbridge, for whom academic study was too often tied to a medieval conception of university life. However, the Japanese did not care for the discursive style of classical German university instruction (even in putatively natural scientific subjects) or the patterns of dependency that it created between professor and fledgling researcher. Instead, they preferred the routinized and 'hands-on' curricular plans of engineering degrees at the polytechnics. They enabled students to pick up necessary skills and then go on with their lives. Japanese students overseas would often remark on the low status that the Germans themselves ascribed to what struck them as an obviously more efficient and empowering form of instruction.[25]

Recall that the liberal arts basis of the Western university prejudiced it against the inclusion of laboratory-based subjects until shortly before the Japanese themselves became interested in those subjects. The 'liberal arts' literally meant subjects that can be done without using one's hands – the mark of a free person. The university was conceived as a place for aristocrats, clerics, and civil servants to learn how to think and speak well, and those goals dictated a discipline's relative value. By their heavy reliance on machinery, the artisan-like character of their work, and their inevitable sensory assaults (i.e. foul sights, sounds, and odours), the laboratory based natural sciences were marked as lower-class endeavours. Consequently, the major European scientists before 1850 who spent their careers in universities typically held chairs in mathematics or natural philosophy. The rest worked in polytechnics, hospitals, or in autonomous institutions like the Royal Society, where class distinctions were less crucial. (And, of course, some, like Charles Darwin, lived on their inheritance.) In 1825, Justus Liebig (1803–73) managed to establish a chemistry laboratory at a marginal German university, but it was only after a recently united but technically superior Germany trounced France in the 1870 Franco–Prussian War that the European nations came around to the idea that the natural sciences ought to be brought from the polytechnics into the universities and made part of general education. Thereafter laboratories were increasingly located on university grounds and used not only for research but for teaching as well. From that standpoint, the Japanese were hardly catching up, as the Imperial University of Tokyo was founded in 1877 with the natural sciences and engineering as its centrepiece. In fact, Japan was arguably the first nation in the world to implement a nationwide policy for science education and research.

We can get a good sense of the still relatively immature state of Europe's scientific infrastructure in the first decade of the twentieth century by looking at what impressed Europeans about the Japanese. In his 1903 presidential address to the Royal Society, entitled, 'The influence of brain power in history', the astronomer Norman Lockyer (1836–1920) pointed to Japan's unprecedented ability to harness science to national, not simply personal, needs. When it looked like the Japanese were beating the Russians in their 1905 war, *Nature* published an editorial calling for the European nations to boost their provision of scientific research and training for all its citizens. Indeed, *Nature* decried the uneven development of science in Europe as a source of its major social problems, as the concentration of scientific knowledge in the hands of elites, be they located in universities or polytechnics, threatened to recreate old class divisions.[26]

Lest we think that this call to arms was unique to Britain, a country notorious for the individualist cast of its scientific innovators, it turns out that the situation was only marginally better in

Germany. The image of the late nineteenth-century German professor commanding a hierarchy of academic underlings to work on
well defined problems that contribute to an overall disciplinary trajectory is partly anachronistic. A more accurate picture would note
the continuities with the medieval practice of students gravitating
around a 'master' whose reputation for wide learning and wisdom
was matched only by his idiosyncrasy of vision. That a professor
could gather students and resources around him testified only to his
charisma and entrepreneurship, and not necessarily to his contribution to some larger body of scientific knowledge.[27] Most German
professors were *de facto* philosophers whose technological needs
had managed to keep pace with industrialization. Needless to say,
incommensurability between the various German departments and
laboratories was widely noted and criticized at the time. Interestingly, the intervention of the state was often crucial in supporting
the role of professional associations in the enforcement of common
educational standards and the adoption of common textbooks, two
necessary ingredients for the sort of 'normal science' that Kuhn
claimed to be necessary for knowledge to be truly cumulative.[28]

Under the circumstances, the USA came closer to providing an
adequate blueprint for the design of Japan's research and educational policy. In 1862 President Abraham Lincoln (1809–65) had
signed into law the Morrill Act, which established the first 'land-
grant' universities. These institutions of higher learning were
largely designed to produce knowledge in the agricultural and
industrial arts that could be readily transmitted to inhabitants of the
university vicinity. Large laboratories and 'research stations' were
the focal points of academic activity, often with ready access to
farms and factories, while the status of traditional liberal arts subjects was reduced to providing 'service' courses in basic literacy and
numeracy. The first Superintendent of Schools and Colleges in
Japan, David Murray (1830–1905), was a major administrator and
theorist of land-grant institutions. However, in the end, the US
system revealed faults not dissimilar to those of the German
system. On the one hand, the historical fragmentation of the
German principalities made it difficult to coordinate the administration of educational policy in the newly unified Germany. The
result was a highly competitive but disorganized academic culture
which enabled each professor to lord over his disciplinary fiefdom
with virtual impunity. On the other hand, the US Constitution

offered principled resistance to the idea of a unified educational policy by endorsing the rights of local authorities to dictate curricular matters. Here the highly centralized and stratified French educational system seemed the best model for Japan's nation-building purposes.[29]

Most of the European advisers hired by the Japanese cautioned against the promotion of scientific training that was not securely grounded in what Kant had called the 'public' use of reason. Kant's original idea was the Enlightenment one of people participating in decisions that are taken to apply their knowledge. They would be no mere technicians serving another master's ends, but knowledgeable agents who would share responsibility for the situations in which their expertise played a role. However, as the Kantian ideal was institutionalized in the modern German university, students of the natural sciences and engineering had first to be trained in the humanistic subjects of philosophy, history, and the arts to ensure that the appropriate value orientation – one friendly to Western (more specifically, Prussian-national) sensibilities about democracy, open-mindedness, and criticism – is transmitted. Aside from an obvious concern with the Japanese possibly using their newly learned technical skills against the West, the European advisers also believed that the spirit of scientific innovation would not be sustained unless Japan acquired the cultural context in which such a spirit had developed in the West. Certainly, the historical schemes of Hegel, Comte, and Spencer made it clear that the genius of Galileo, Newton, and Faraday was due more to the Renaissance, Enlightenment, and Victorian cultures in which they were embedded than to anything that could be explained by their work alone.

For their part, the Japanese were bemused that modern Europeans could believe in such a superstitious sense of historical destiny. They were much more impressed with that most original of Western impulses, namely, the Greek one of opportunistically borrowing from other cultures, improving on what is borrowed, and then using it to gain the respect of those cultures.[30] Thus, when Europeans offered advice on what to do about the prospect of students taking offence at Darwinism and other scientific theories that challenged traditional religious (i.e. Judaeo–Christian) conceptions, the Japanese observed that they had not encountered the West's ideological difficulties with the original 'revolutionary' scientific theory, Copernicanism, once it was introduced as part of

Newtonian mechanics in the late eighteenth century. This was mainly because the Confucian basis of Japanese culture did not invest any overriding cosmological significance in the idea of an Earth-centred universe. While Confucianism holds that each thing has its 'governing centre', it does not hold that everything has the *same* such centre. Consequently, it was possible for the Japanese to harbour a 'multiple truth' conception of reality that would not have sat well with either Galileo or his Inquisitors, but would nevertheless have avoided the need for any scientific revolution to take place. In that sense, Japan enjoyed the advantage of not having to overcome centuries-old Western cultural barriers to the development of the natural sciences.

Here it is interesting to compare Japan's assimilation of Western science in the century prior to the Meiji Restoration with the Muslim and Christian reception of the Greek scientific tradition in the Middle Ages. Muslim scholars struggled to systematize the ancient Greek scientific corpus – usually as seen through Aristotelian eyes – by carefully reproducing in Arabic as much of the original Greek conceptual framework as possible. Thus, many new distinctions were drawn that had not previously existed in Muslim thought, but that would come to dominate it for several centuries. However, because Greek science was itself not all cut from the same cloth, the ensuing attempts at reconciling contradictory claims led to considerable philosophical speculation and debate, the intensity of which was compounded by the fact that the Greek tradition ultimately had to be rendered compatible with the teachings of the Qur'an. The Christian scholastics who directly benefited from these Muslim efforts continued along much the same lines, only this time in Latin, and with the added burden of having to identify and counter blasphemous doctrines with which the Muslim scholars were thought to have leavened their syntheses.[31] The only 'advantage' enjoyed by the scholastics – at least from the standpoint of the subsequent history of science – was that the Church was not sufficiently organized to impose an ideological orthodoxy.

In the case of Japan, although it had officially closed its doors to the West, European scientific texts made their way into the country via Dutch traders in China. However, the importation was piecemeal, and no pretence was made to fashion the imported knowledge into a seamless whole, let alone weave it into the fabric of Japanese culture. The Japanese word for the European conception of science, *kagaku*, stressed exclusively science's instrumental and productive character.[32] Because Western science was recognized at all times as irreducibly alien, the Japanese were able to treat, say, Newtonian mechanics as a set of tools for certain purposes, but not others, and thus physics was never perceived as a generalized threat to traditional cultural beliefs and values. This point was only underscored by the dominance of the exact sciences by the *samurai* in the first half century of modernization. In contrast, medicine, one of the last disciplines in the West to be introduced to the ways of modern science, was the main source of the relatively few philosophical controversies in the history of Japanese science. This was largely due to a combination of Confucianism's anthropocentric orientation, which gave medicine an intellectual status it lacked in the West, as well as the discipline's access to commoners as a vehicle for social mobility.[33]

Perhaps the best symbol of Japan's circumvention of European history was the rewriting of technical scientific terms in ideographic script. Whereas Western science students are still forced to confront their increasingly remote Graeco–Roman roots every time they tried to decipher the meaning of a technical term, Japanese students could simply read the meaning from the ideogram, which would depict the main properties of the element or process to which the term refers. The person most responsible for this move was Shizuki Tadao (1760–1806), who first rendered Newton in Japanese, but not by what was then the usual method of phonetic translation into Chinese sound characters. That would mean having Japanese students learn neologisms that sound like Newton's original English (or Latin, in the case of *Philosophiae Naturalis Principiu Mathematica*, 1687) but which have no clear place in the semantic universe of the Japanese language. Such a translation strategy would have only made Newtonian concepts more alien to Japanese students than Latinate words like 'gravity' and 'inertia' are to modern European students. Instead, Shizuki selected ideograms that constituted primitive operational definitions of Newton's concepts. For example, 'gravity' was depicted as 'power to create weight'. The distinctly instrumental spin to Shizuki's rendition of Newtonian mechanics managed to avoid protracted discussions of the ontological status of gravity and inertia that continued to haunt philosophically oriented Western physicists, such as Mach and Albert Einstein (1879–1955), even as Japan was mobilizing its scientific forces in the late 19th century. More importantly, it helped to open up scientific training to the vast majority of the student population who were unfamiliar with European language and culture.[34]

Although the Japanese modernizers were generally unmoved by fears of profaning traditional culture, a somewhat related worry emerged from the Meiji emperor's Confucian adviser, who had noticed the historical tendency of science to destabilize traditional forms of authority in the West. Would not the same happen in Japan? Here Prime Minister Ito Hirobumi (1841–1909) took a lesson from the Europeans, although not the one they intended. The Confucian adviser read the history of Western science as Westerners themselves often do, namely, as a story of critical inquiry gradually overcoming the barriers strewn on its path by tradition. If Japanese scientists adopted a similar mindset, and developed a taste for pushing back the frontiers of knowledge rather than simply applying knowledge to national needs, then Japan would soon lose its distinctive cultural identity. Such a prospect was what the Confucian adviser feared and the European advisers desired. However, Ito realized that this sense of history presupposed that the social role of the scientist was still that of the heroic individual – epitomized by Galileo – who directly confronted the social order with his revolutionary theories. The nationalization of science had put an end to those days in the West, especially in the most scientifically advanced country, Germany. In its place had emerged a self-policing group of professionals who treated 'freedom of inquiry' as a guild right to work on narrowly focused topics of no direct relevance, and hence no direct threat, to the larger social order. At the same time, the demand for research publication enabled applied scientists and policy makers to cull the results of these 'free' inquiries for their own purposes. In that sense, Germany's 'Iron Chancellor' Otto von Bismarck (1815–98) could be credited with having turned the universities into a safety valve for overheated intellectuals clamouring for political reform. In effect, the prime minister told his Confucian adviser not to worry: look at what the Westerners do, and not at what they say they do.[35]

Recalling the distinction introduced in Chapter 3, the Japanese were adept at sorting out the West's Enlightenment myth from what had become science's underlying Positivist reality. However, the more astute observers of the occidental scene realized that, however much Positivism rendered academics docile servants of the state, the parochialism of its guild mentality was not necessarily the most efficient way to harness the work of science to the task of nation-building. Several of the designers of Japan's scientific institutions had studied under highly accomplished European and American researchers who were constantly running into trouble for ignoring disciplinary jurisdictions and blurring the professional, the public, and the private. Particularly instructive was the stormy career of Germany's answer to Pasteur, Robert Koch (1843–1910), the man who isolated the micro-organisms responsible for anthrax, tuberculosis, and cholera. Koch was Professor of Hygiene at the University of Berlin but regarded autonomous disciplines as more a hindrance than a help to his medical research. When Koch first thought he had isolated the bacterial cause of tuberculosis, he was prohibited from testing the hypothesis in his own laboratory, but had to turn the job over to colleagues in the Department of Clinical Medicine.

Koch's untested hypothesis immediately became a token in German academic politics. On the one hand, the Ministry of Education tried to score an international public relations coup by announcing that the Germans had arrived at a cure for the great modern health scourge that tuberculosis was. On the other hand, Koch's own colleagues in anatomy and physiology dismissed the very idea that disease could be the result of anything other than some sort of bodily imbalance. After all, to admit that disease could be caused by foreign agents would challenge the notion that the human body constitutes a completely autonomous sphere of inquiry. Some old dogs would have to start to learn some new tricks. Not surprisingly, Koch soon resigned his professorship to set up a laboratory under the auspices of the Imperial Health Office, which ironically secured him more independence by remaining open to a variety of external influences but colonized by none of them. Koch's premier Japanese student, Kitasato Shibashiburo (1852–1931), established a similar laboratory when he returned home, and spent the rest of his career avoiding an over-scrupulous observance to what we would now mark as the distinction between 'basic' and 'applied' research. But even more importantly, Kitasato promoted the idea that science best served the national interest by promoting criticism that crossed all institutional boundaries. Eventually, this sentiment forced him to resign from government service and to

secure entirely private funding for his Institute for Infectious Dis-
eases.[36]

It was not long before humanists in the metropolitan powers
acknowledged the implications of Japan's selective appropriation
of Western science. By 1905 the 'uniqueness' of Western science
was conceptualized as a matter of *contingency*, as if it were only by
accident that the natural sciences had emerged in Europe rather
than in, say, China, India, or Egypt. The force of this point was to
suggest *both* that the natural sciences were within any culture's
reach *and* that Europe's domination of the globe was by no means
guaranteed in perpetuity. Thus, the first victory in the long war
against eurocentrism had been scored.[37] Scholarly interest in
science's place in history shifted from science as the reflection of
more general European attitudes, to science as a relatively autonomous enterprise that was easily exported (through imperialism) or
imported (by Japan). Here it is worth recalling that imperial expansion was often promoted as a way of addressing (or at least divert-
ing attention from) signs of economic and cultural decline that were
already occurring at home. Little surprise, then, that France was the
country in which history of science was first recognized as a field of
inquiry, since it was the major European power most publicly preoccupied with the prospect of succumbing to the type of 'degener-
ation' that threatened to turn it into the new 'sick man of Europe',
a title that had come to be associated with the Ottoman Empire.
Thus, history of science became the last stand of French culture on
the world-historic stage.[38]

When Japan first took to the world stage in 1869, Western intellectuals argued that the Japanese would not be able to match the
West's scientific achievement unless they also reproduced the cultural background against which that achievement had occurred. In
philosophy of science terms, they held that the Japanese would
need to retrace the West's 'discovery' process in order for its scientific knowledge to be fully 'justified'. However, the Japanese constructed alternative means to their desired scientific ends; in some
cases capitalizing on their metaphysical and religious differences
with the West, while in other cases hybridizing Western institutions
and practices. Once Japan defeated Russia without the supposed
epistemic prerequisites, Westerners reworked the essence of
science so that it no longer required a knowledge of philosophy and
the other arts subjects. If this historical tendency continues, then it

is safe to assume that there is no essence to science, no transcendental core to knowledge, without which contact with reality would be impossible. The Japanese showed that with a little ingenuity, there is almost always a way to adapt domestic forms of knowledge to avoid the cultural costs of importing foreign ones. The more general lesson for students of science is this: knowledge that survives multiple cross-cultural translations is simply the residual product of those translations and does not require any further metaphysical explanation for its persistence. This is not to deny the potential value of *wanting* to standardize knowledge across cultures. However, this desire has to be understood as being of a *political* nature. Depending on the situation, such standardization may serve to dissolve or establish social hierarchies, either within or between societies.

Generalizing from the Japanese experience, a distinction can be drawn in the distribution of costs and benefits in cross-cultural translation. In short, we may stress the convenience of either the *producer* or the *consumer* of knowledge. The former has a natural interest in promoting a form of knowledge that is as uniform as possible across contexts of use, ideally to the point that potential consumers are willing to adjust their interests in order to acquire that knowledge. An extreme case is to require a mastery of Newtonian mechanics before someone can practice engineering, which means that anyone with the desire to build something must possess the same physical theory. On a more ordinary scale, adherence to expert advice and the personal acquisition of educational credentials, especially when they appear to defer the immediate satisfaction of one's interests, are also examples in which consumers bend to the will of the producers. Consumers, for their part, have a natural interest in possessing a form of knowledge that capitalizes as much as possible on what they already know and want, even if that means reducing knowledge to a customized good that varies across consumer interests and lays no claims to challenging consumption patterns. The extreme case here is the 'expert system', a computer that is programmed with an expert's knowledge of some subject, to which the client then has access via a 'user-friendly' interface, especially designed with the client's needs in mind.[39] In sum, the knowledge producer's standpoint is *transcendental:* conceiving of knowledge as something without which one's goal cannot be reached. In contrast, the knowledge consumer's standpoint is

Translation poles	Knowledge producer	Knowledge consumer
Standpoint	Transcendental	Economical
Knowledge is . . .	Necessary condition	Necessary evil
Aim is to . . .	Maximize need for knowledge	Minimize need for knowledge
Translation field	Monopolistic	Competitive
Ideal case	Grand unified theory	Customized expert system
Nineteenth century example	Europe and the USA	Japan

Figure 6.2   Knowledge producers and knowledge consumers.

economical, which means that knowledge is ultimately seen as a cost that must be borne but should be minimized as much as possible, a necessary evil rather than a necessary condition.[40] These differences are encapsulated in Figure 6.2.

Notes

1 Said (1978).
2 For a critical discussion of this tendency, see Ahmad (1992).
3 For a nuanced comparison of China's and Islam's relationship to the development of science in Europe, stressing the trade patterns among these cultures, see Goodman and Russell (1991: 7–17). Although Needham argued that the West owed its impetus for studying magnetism and immunology to the Chinese, there is little direct evidence to support this hypothesis, thereby leaving the 'controlled experiment' image of his comparison of China and the West largely intact.
4 My discussion of Islamic revivalism draws primarily upon Rahman (1982), Al-Azmeh (1993), and Rahmena (1994).
5 Here I follow Andre Gunder Frank's recent revision of world-systems theory. See Frank (1995); Bergesen (1995).
6 Sivin (1982: 47–51). This point would not have surprised the man who introduced the expression 'Scientific Revolution' into English shortly after the Second World War, Herbert Butterfield, since his benchmark of a revolution was the message of Jesus Christ, the institutionalization of which was achieved only with great difficulty over the course of several centuries.
7 Zeldin (1967).
8 Inkster (1991: 97).
9 Johnson (1990: 43).

10 Lewis (1982: 135–70).
11 Barnett (1967).
12 Crabbs (1984: 87–108); Halsey (1992: 63).
13 Graff (1987: 374–81).
14 Bouzid (1996). The intellectual vigour of recent debates over 'Islamic science' can be witnessed in Sardar (1989).
15 The difference between Islam and the West on this point is not quite as stark as I have made it out to be. For example, Plato would probably have had an easier time relating to the Muslim sensibility than to today's Western one because he presumed a natural correspondence between the True and the Good. However, Plato also believed that access to this unified vision was restricted to an elite. This view turned out to be better suited to the disorganized state of Christendom, as the reception of Averroës well illustrates.
16 Duhem (1913).
17 Keddie (1968).
18 Brooke (1991: 96).
19 Ben-David (1984: 71).
20 Kuhn (1977: 21–30, 240–65).
21 Ralston (1990: 43–78).
22 Ralston (1990: 142–72).
23 Morris-Suzuki (1994).
24 Bartholomew (1989: 35–62).
25 Bartholomew (1989: 63–82).
26 Inkster (1991: 184–204). The book is generally an excellent source for pursuing the Gerschenkron thesis discussed in Chapter 5.
27 Ben-David (1984: 108–38). As a devotee of 'free market' economics, Ben-David fails to register the down side of this approach, from the standpoint of contributing to a body of knowledge that can serve the larger society.
28 Kuhn (1977: 220). Here Kuhn was trying to correct the image he left in *The Structure of Scientific Revolutions* that all the ingredients of normal science had been in place as early as the seventeenth century, if not earlier.
29 Bartholomew (1989: 95–8); Inkster (1991: 126).
30 This is a polite way of putting the thesis of Bernal (1987). One should keep in mind that Japan's cultural compass had been traditionally oriented towards China, which typically treated foreigner influences as potentially destabilizing the harmony between culture and nature.
31 Grant (1977: Chap. 2).
32 Bartholomew (1989: 4); Inkster (1991: 189).
33 Bartholomew (1989: 44–5).
34 Montgomery (1995: Chap. 5).
35 Bartholomew (1989: 103–4).

36 Bartholomew (1989: 81–2, 102, 166–8).
37 Pyenson (1993a).
38 Pyenson (1993b).
39 Fuller (1994c).
40 There have been some limited but promising cases in which Third
    World nations have reversed the producer–consumer relationship with
    the West by designing institutions of higher education and research that
    forgo disciplinary divisions unique to the history of European science in
    favour of categories that play more directly to native strengths. These
    include 'rice studies' (Philippines), 'rubber technology' (Malaysia), and
    'tropical science' (Costa Rica). From a European perspective they are
    relatively marginal 'interdisciplinary' areas of study, but from the native
    perspective they are autonomous fields of inquiry sporting their own
    international journals in which Westerners are eager to publish. On this
    and other strategies for 'capacity-building' in Third World science
    policy, see Shahidullah (1991).

7

Science as the Standard of Civilization: Does it have a Future?

Why did a 'Scientific Revolution' occur in seventeenth-century Europe – or why did the 'Leap of Thales' occur in sixth century BC Greece – instead of somewhere with a comparable or even superior standard of civilization, such as China or Egypt? Popular science writers, not least professional scientists writing in that capacity, continue to be captivated by this question. That multiculturalists have come to target the question as ripe for deconstruction is only the latest testimony to the hold that it has on our imaginations. Living in the twilight of the twentieth century, we may be embarrassed by the presumptuousness of what it asks, as if non-European peoples collectively *lacked* some quality that turned out to be of world-historic importance. However, unpacking the three assumptions built into the question, we see that the question, while undeniably eurocentric, is motivated by a precarious sense of Europe's standing in human history.

1 An entire civilization can be judged by the development of its natural scientific knowledge.
2 The pivotal event in the history of science need not have occurred when and where it did, if at all.
3 Once the event did occur somewhere in Europe, it could not occur anywhere else, except *through* Europe.

Compare the prominence given to contingency in our question –

how easily things could have been otherwise – with, say, the tale of
linear progress recounted in Hegel's *Philosophy of History* (1830)
of the early nineteenth century. According to Hegel, the *Weltgeist*
never looked back as it marched out of an Oriental Past into an
Occidental Future. But then again, Hegel did not see the collection
of disciplines we now call the natural sciences as the decisive civilizing force. Indeed, he was rather derisive of that icon of scientific
revolutionaries, Newton. Instead, Hegel identified the trajectory of
history with a peculiarly Prussian rendition of the path from dic-
tatorship to democracy that was popularized in the Enlightenment.
Like most of his contemporaries and immediate successors, Hegel
sought the state of civilization in the overall character of the social
order, not in some specific feature of the society, such as the state
of its natural science. Consequently, the question of whether Egypt
or China could have borne the decisive civilizing force would have
struck Hegel as unintelligible. *By definition*, it could not have done
so, because these societies were instances of *Oriental Despotism* –
an expression that will haunt us throughout this chapter. What,
then, shook Europeans from Hegel's dogmatism, causing them at
the same time to identify the crux of Western civilization with the
natural sciences? In Chapter 6, we suggested that the 1905
Russo–Japanese War was a pivotal event. However, any systematic
search for an answer must consider the history of international law,
where *the standard of civilization* makes its first official appearance
in 1836 in Henry Wheaton's (1783–1848) *Elements of International
Law*.[1]

Wheaton introduced the standard as a consolation prize for the
lack of an enforceable universal law of nations. The standard was
explicitly eurocentric in defining a civilized nation as one that pro-
tected the 'life, liberty, and property' of its European residents.
Legal scholars were well aware that it would be difficult for a nation
to meet this standard without the natives adjusting themselves to a
European way of life. However, what convinced Wheaton and his
colleagues that the standard was not completely self-serving were
the contrasting paths taken by Russia and Turkey over the previous
100 years. On the one hand, Peter the Great had deliberately set
out to Westernize Russia, most notably by establishing a Russian
Academy of Science, which for many years was populated primarily
by foreigners. On the other hand, the palpable decline of the
Ottoman Empire seemed to result from its engagement in a series

of debilitating internal wars, while increasingly ignoring its historical ties to the rest of Europe. What impressed legal scholars about these two cases was the unequivocal consequences of nations taking it upon themselves to adopt and reject European culture, respectively. Scholars were therefore able to avoid the feats of casuistry that had been required in the sixteenth and seventeenth centuries to justify Christian conquistadores forcing the European way of being upon uncooperative native Americans.

That Peter the Great would embark on an ambitious and arduous campaign to bring Russia in line with the rest of Europe strongly implied that Europe had produced something worth emulating. But what exactly was its distinctive contribution to humanity? The credibility of a Judaeo–Christian basis for international law had been severely strained since the French Revolution, so legal scholars sought a more naturalistic grounding that catered to the Positivist spirit of the day. This led to a spate of attempts to define civilization in terms of race, climate, and customs. However, none of these seemed to capture shifting European intuitions about who was and was not civilized. Moreover, the British were especially concerned that tying the standard of civilization too closely to a non-negotiable quality like race could be bad for business, a serious consideration in a time of overseas capital expansion: who cares what colour people are, if they are prepared to buy your goods? These worries came to a head as Japan became a world power, after barely a generation of modernization. While some Enlightenment wits had predicted the long-term ascendancy of the USA over Europe on the grounds that the USA lacked such atavistic European institutions as the absolute monarchy and the landed aristocracy, they would not have anticipated Japan's success, since it started precisely with these political and economic 'liabilities' but quickly refashioned them to raise the country's international status.

Henceforth, debates over the standard of civilization shifted focus from the necessity of Europe as such to the necessity of 'something' that by historical accident began in Europe. As to be expected of world capitalist culture, that 'something' was defined by what the ascendant non-Europeans seemed to want most from the Europeans. Thus, the standard of civilization could be read off the balance sheet of cultural exchange. In this way, the natural sciences and technology replaced art, literature, and philosophy as the relevant standard. In short, to peg the standard of civilization to the

	Overdetermined	*Underdetermined*
Retrospective	East fell behind	East was never in the race
Prospective	West may lose the lead (the East becomes the leader in science)	West may stop the race (science declines as the West declines)

Figure 7.1   Plotting the end of science.

development of the natural sciences is to see the significance of European culture as non-Europeans do. That Europeans would be drawn to accept this image as their own testifies to just how much the West adapted to circumstances beyond its control. Basically, the appeal to the natural sciences as the mark of civilization was a last-ditch effort to shore up the claim to European uniqueness before the claim was rendered completely implausible.[2]

To put it in the terms introduced in Chapter 5, as the twentieth century has caused modernist views of the human condition to yield to postmodernist ones, the source of the contingency associated with the rise of science in the West has shifted from its initial 'overdeterminationist' interpretation to its current 'underdeterminationist' one. Instead of stressing that the West need not have been the leader in science, historians are now more likely to claim that there need not have been a 'science' in which the West has so clearly excelled since the seventeenth century. But whether one adopts an over- or underdeterminationist framework, the decline of science in the West can be just as easily posed as its rise. Where Needham posed the retrospective question of why the Scientific Revolution began in Europe and not Asia, we can prospectively ask why the Scientific Revolution may end in Europe and not Asia.

If, in the overdeterminationist view, the Chinese lost the 'race' to the Scientific Revolution, then it is entirely possible that the West will relinquish its lead in the future to, say, Japan or the Far East more generally. But if, as the underdeterminationist reading implies, the Chinese were never in the science race in the first place, then correspondingly the West may drop out in the future. The question, of course, would remain as to whether this latter possibility would herald the 'end of science' altogether. But how might such a thing come about?

While any answer to this question is bound to be speculative, one good indicator is that the social functions jointly satisfied by the pursuit of scientific knowledge would come to be individually satisfied in separate practices. The university was crucial for the advancement of science in the West mainly because it provided a common space for the production and distribution of knowledge (through the university's research and teaching functions, respectively) that permitted an intellectual synergy to develop between the demands of innovation and tradition. In the thirteenth century, academics began to take a professional interest in why craft innovations worked as well as they did; by the end of the nineteenth century they found themselves in the business of producing such innovations, often on a large scale, in the case of chemistry. Given the recent 'market-driven' challenges to the institutional integrity of the university, it is easy to imagine, on the one hand, the privatization of innovation as intellectual property and, on the other, the formalization of tradition through vocational certification. The former function would be increasingly performed by entrepreneurs and their industrial backers, while the latter would be left to academics, whose courses of study and examinations would determine who can enter which field of employment. As the production and distribution of scientific knowledge grow steadily apart in this fashion, we could witness a quick reversal of the past 700 years of Western history.

An important sign of this reversal would be that the meanings of words associated with 'science', and 'knowledge' more generally, start losing their clarity. 'Science' may slide into the semantic space of 'religion' and refer more to a set of institutions and rituals than a set of theories and methods. As educational standards fragment, 'knowing' may come to signify specific social practices like 'verifying' or 'certifying,' or it may devolve into a casual word, like 'coping' and 'adapting'. Yesterday's oxymorons turn into tomorrow's platitudes. In Chapter 4, the Martian anthropologists identified a prominent clue that the end of science may be near – the popularity of Derek de Solla Price's expression *Big Science*, Orwellian Newspeak that, since its debut in the early 1960s, has come to mean 'great science'.[3] 'Big Science' literally refers to expensive research projects, first in physics and chemistry and more recently in molecular biology, that are affordable only by the more affluent nations but on which all nations increasingly set their sights. This global fixation on Big Science has obscured the fact that in the past great science was what Kuhn called 'revolutionary science', cheap in its conduct but dear in its consequences – yet not so dear as to discourage the revolutionary impulse altogether. The desire to complete the 'big picture' put forth by a Newton, Darwin, or Einstein has required the mass retraining of scientists in new techniques and methods, new ways of seeing the world, and sometimes the development of new instruments of investigation. This reorientation, while invariably resisted by the scientific orthodoxy, was at least financially tolerable. But as science has come to be so thoroughly involved in the economic and political maintenance of the societies housing its pursuit, any truly revolutionary project in science today would pose as great a threat to societal stability as a political revolution normally would. While the diminishing half-life of scientific journal literature is indicative of a rapidly advancing research frontier ('Price's Index'), all of this activity nevertheless occurs over a relatively small set of issues, reflecting the need to make the most of science's fixed capital resources.

In Chapter 1, I suggested that recent events point to science entering a *post-epistemic mode*, one in which (as our Martian friends would put it) the 'industrial' side of science's military–industrial metaphor completely eclipses the 'military' side. As the potentially critical function of scientific inquiry is channelled into a narrow bandwidth of technical discourse, any residue of this carefully contained criticism can be used to legitimate and reproduce society's status quo. This transition may be modelled on the long discredited idea of Oriental Despotism, which draws on Hegel's and Marx's dystopic portrayal of Eastern regimes known as 'the Asiatic mode of production'.[4] Accordingly, the dominant class does not own the means of production but instead controls the state and economy through its ability to extract rents from villagers and landholders, which are then used to finance large-scale public works projects. In our emerging 'information-based', 'knowledge-intensive' society, the new 'rents' are the training costs that students must incur in order to possess the credentials required for being employable (if not actually employed). In such a world, academics shift completely from being producers of innovative, potentially disruptive knowledge to being gatekeepers of the processes of societal reproduction. In return, the fees paid by students feed into the proprietary research that academics are increasingly encouraged to pursue in cooperation with industry. Most of what transpires in such research is ultimately not intended for classroom consumption. Indeed, depending on the legal protection under which the research is covered, its fruits may entirely lose their status as 'public goods', which would in turn raise the spectre of 'fields of knowledge' being quite literally mapped, ploughed, and mined in a system of legal relations that one commentator has not unfairly dubbed *information feudalism*.[5]

This book began with a survey showing that the public lacks a coherent understanding of science. People could appreciate the work done by particular disciplines but they could not see what those disciplines had in common. With that in mind, let us now briefly return to the paradigm case of Oriental Despotism, medieval China, and its most prominent polymath, Shen Kua (1031–95).[6] At one level, Shen resembled the archetypal 'Renaissance man', Leonardo da Vinci (1452–1519), in his voracious intellectual appetites and substantive contributions to mathematics, astronomy, cartography, geology, meteorology, magnetics, engineering, economics, and medicine – not to mention several works on religious matters. However, Shen did not seem to regard his activities as closed under a single conceptual rubric such as 'science' or 'philosophy'. In his memoirs, for example, he organized the various projects he did for the imperial bureaucracy in terms of their practical contexts rather than any overarching principles. Moreover, while he clearly mastered and improved upon a great many fields of knowledge, he treated each as self-contained and typically tolerated contradictions between the fundamental principles of the different fields, often invoking the ultimately inaccessible or mysterious character of reality. It simply did not occur to Shen to try to mediate conflicting bodies of thought through critical inquiry.

We may marvel that someone as obviously intelligent and accomplished as Shen Kua never manifested what we now consider to be the core scientific impulse. Yet, are we not moving in the same direction today, as an increasing proportion of academics are forced by continual funding needs to do contract research that over time involve the mastery of a variety of disparate 'project areas'? For his part, Shen Kua could fall back on Confucianism and Taoism to justify the futility of attaining synthetic or universal knowledge. Today's academics have no problem explaining the fractal character of their curricula vitae in terms of the 'postmodern condition', whereby what the Chinese had metaphysically shrouded in 'flux' is now openly embraced as 'flexibility'. The most reassuring feature of this analogy is that our current predicament appears as a phase in a recognizable cycle through which humanity shall eventually pass. But it would be even more reassuring to learn from the past, so that science does not diminish itself as it enhances the society that promotes its pursuit. In that case, the first lesson is that the mark of science is to be found, not in its products, but in the spirit in which they are produced.

Notes

1 Gong (1984: 20–53).
2 Pyenson (1993b).
3 Crowther (1968: 317–20).
4 Wittfogel (1957). The concept is applied to the history of science in Dorn (1991).
5 Drahos (1995).
6 Sivin (1982: 47–51).

Suggested Reading

These are meant to provide background to readers who are thinking about the social character of scientific knowledge for the first time and wish to explore the full range of perspectives currently on the market. Montgomery (1995) is a good general introduction to the internal diversity of the sciences, especially highlighting the role that language has played in constituting the scientific identity. The democratization of knowledge as a theme in the history of the natural and social sciences is comprehensively surveyed in Proctor (1991), with Delanty (1997) providing an excellent survey of contemporary trends. On social epistemology, readers can consult the references to my own writings, or (perhaps better for beginners) Taylor (1996) and Collier (1997). Both are designed as textbooks, the former aimed at humanities students and the latter at science students. Social epistemology draws upon the history, philosophy, and sociology of science, fields which are presented best when presented together. This is the ideal espoused by the emerging interdisciplinary field of science and technology studies, to which all of the above works dedicate some significant discussion. More specifically, on history and philosophy of science, I strongly recommend Hacking (1982) and Gjertsen (1989) as texts. As for sociology of science, Latour and Woolgar (1986), the classic ethnography of scientists in their 'native habitat', is a masterpiece of defamiliarization and hence worth a peek, if only for stylistic reasons. Gilbert and Mulkay (1984) remains the best book explaining how one actually does sociology of science. Readers should also dip into the journal, *Social Studies of Science*, for the most recent empirical developments in the field. On science and multiculturalism, the best collection in terms of sheer coverage and democratic orientation is Harding (1993). In this area, readers should take care to canvass a variety of viewpoints. Huff (1993) and Hess (1995) provide a nice contrast, as the former applies a broadly Mertonian perspective to understanding the uniqueness of Western science, while the latter takes a line somewhat closer to the one in these pages.

References

Adams, H. (ed.) (1971) *Critical Theory since Plato*. New York: Harcourt Brace Jovanovich.

Ahmad, A. (1992) *In Theory: Classes, Nations, Literatures*. London: Verso.

Ainslie, G. (1992) *Picoeconomics*. Cambridge: Cambridge University Press.

Al-Azmeh, A. (1993) *Islams and Modernities*. London: Verso.

Aron, R. (1957) *The Opium of the Intellectuals*. Garden City, NY: Doubleday.

Arndt, H. W. (1978) *Economic Development: The History of an Idea*. Chicago, IL: University of Chicago Press.

Barnett, C. (1967) 'The education of military elites', in W. Laqueur and G. Mosse (eds) *Education and Social Structure in the Twentieth Century*. New York: Harper & Row.

Bartholomew, J. (1989) *The Formation of Science in Japan*. New Haven, CT: Yale University Press.

Baudrillard, J. (1983) *Simulations*. New York: Semiotexte.

Bazerman, C. (1987) *Shaping Written Knowledge*. Madison, WI: University of Wisconsin Press.

Beck, U. (1992) *The Risk Society*. London: Sage.

Bell, D. (1973) *The Coming of Post-Industrial Society*. New York: Harper & Row.

Bell, D. (1982) 'The return of the sacred: The argument about the future of religion', in G. Almond, M. Chodorow, and R. Pearce (eds.) *Progress and Its Discontents*. Berkeley, CA: University of California Press.

Ben-David, J. (1984) *The Scientist's Role in Society*, 2nd edn. Chicago, IL: University of Chicago Press.

Ben-David, J. and Collins, R. (1966) 'Social factors in the origin of a new science: The case of psychology', *American Sociological Review* **31**, 451–65.

Bergesen, A. (1995) 'Let's be frank about world history', in S. K. Sanderson (ed.) *Civilizations and World Systems: Studying World-Historical Change*. Walnut Creek, CA: Sage.

Bernal, M. (1987) *Black Athena: The Afroasiatic Roots of Classical Civilization*. New Brunswick, NJ: Rutgers University Press.

Bouzid, A. (1996) 'Science and technology in the discourse of Sayyid Qutb', *Social Epistemology* **10**, 289–304.

Brooke, J. H. (1991) *Science and Religion*. Cambridge: Cambridge University Press.

Brown, R. (1984) *The Nature of Social Laws*. Cambridge: Cambridge University Press.

Brush, S. (1975) 'Should the history of science be rated X?', *Science* **183**, 1164–83.

Butterfield, H. (1955) *Man on His Past: The Study of the History of Historical Scholarship*. Cambridge: Cambridge University Press.

Campbell, D. and Stanley, J. (1966) *Experimental and Quasi-Experimental Designs for Research*. Chicago, IL: Rand McNally.

Ceccarelli, L. (1995) 'A rhetoric of interdisciplinary scientific discourse: textual criticism of Dobzhansky's *Genetics and the Origins of Species*', *Social Epistemology*, **9**, 91–112.

Chubin, D. and Hackett, E. (1990) *Peerless Science*. Albany, NY: SUNY Press.

Cohen, H. F. (1994) *The Scientific Revolution: A Historiographical Inquiry*. Chicago, IL: University of Chicago Press.

Collier, J. (1997) *Scientific and Technical Communication: Theory, Practice and Policy*. Walnut Creek, CA: Sage.

Collins, H. (1985) *Changing Order*. London: Sage.

Collins, H. (1991) *Artificial Experts*. Cambridge, MA: MIT Press.

Collins, H. and Pinch, T. (1993) *The Golem: What Everyone Should Know about Science*. Cambridge: Cambridge University Press.

Cozzens, S. (1985) 'Comparing the sciences: citation context analysis of papers from neuropharmacology and the sociology of science', *Social Studies of Science*, **15**, 127–53.

Crabbs, J. (1984) *The Writing of History in Nineteenth Century Egypt*. Detroit, MI: Wayne University Press.

Crowther, J. G. (1968) *Science in Modern Society*. New York: Schocken Books.

Dahl, R. (1989) *Democracy and Its Critics*. New Haven, CT: Yale University Press.

Delanty, G. (1997) *Social Science*. Milton Keynes: Open University Press.

De Mey, M. (1982) *The Cognitive Paradigm*. Dordrecht: Kluwer.

Diop, C. A. (1991) *Civilization or Barbarism?* Brooklyn, NY: Lawrence Hill Books.

Dorn, H. (1991) *The Geography of Science*. Baltimore, MD: Johns Hopkins University Press.

Drahos, P. (1995) 'Information feudalism in the information society', *The Information Society*, **11**, 209–22.

Drucker, P. (1993) *Post-Capitalist Society*. New York: HarperCollins.

Duhem, P. (1913) *Le Systeme du Monde*. Paris: Hermann.

Durant, J., Evans, G. and Thomas, G. (1989) 'The public understanding of science', *Nature*, **340**, 11–14.

Eisenstein, E. (1979) *The Printing Press as an Agent of Change*. Cambridge: Cambridge University Press.

Elster, J. (1984) *Sour Grapes*. Cambridge: Cambridge University Press.

Febvre, L. and Martin, H.-J. (1971) *L'apparition du Livre*. Paris: Albin Michel.

Feyerabend, P. (1975) *Against Method*. London: New Left Books.

Feyerabend, P. (1979) *Science in a Free Society*. London: New Left Books.

Frank, A. G. (1995) 'The modern world-system revisited: rereading Braudel and Wallerstein', in S. K. Sanderson (ed.) *Civilizations and World Systems: Studying World Historical Change*. Walnut Creek, CA: Sage.

Frank, R. (1984) 'Are workers paid their marginal products?', *American Economic Review*, **74**, 541–79.

Fukuyama, F. (1992) *The End of History and the Last Man*. New York: Free Press.

Fuller, S. (1988) *Social Epistemology*. Bloomington, IN: Indiana University Press.

Fuller, S. (1993a) *Philosophy of Science and Its Discontents*, 2nd edn. New York: Guilford Press.

Fuller, S. (1993b) *Philosophy, Rhetoric and the End of Knowledge: The Coming of Science & Technology Studies*. Madison, WI: University of Wisconsin Press.

Fuller, S. (1994a) 'The sphere of critical thinking in the post-epistemic world', *Informal Logic*, Winter, 39–54.

Fuller, S. (1994b) 'Rethinking the university from a social constructivist standpoint', *Science Studies*, **7**(1), 4–16.

Fuller, S. (1994c) 'The constitutively social character of expertise', *International Journal of Expert Systems*, **7**, 51–64.

Fuller, S. (1994d) 'Towards a philosophy of science accounting: a critical rendering of instrumental rationality', *Science in Context*, **7**, 591–621.

Fuller, S. (1994e) 'Retrieving the point of realism–instrumentalism debate: Mach vs. Planck on science education policy', in D. Hull *et al.* (eds), *PSA 1994*, vol. 1. East Lansing, MI: Philosophy of Science Association.

Fuller, S. (1996a) 'Talking metaphysical turkey about epistemological chicken', in P. Galison and D. Stump (eds), *The Disunity of Science*. Palo Alto: Stanford University Press.

Fuller, S. (1996b) 'Recent work in social epistemology', *American Philosophical Quarterly*, **33**, 149–66.

Fuller, S. (1996c) 'Social epistemology and the recovery of the normative in the post-epistemic era', *Journal of Mind and Behavior*, **17**, 93–8.

Fuller, S. (1997) 'Society's shifting human–computer interface: a sociology of knowledge for the information age', in M. Henry (ed.) *Computers for Social and Political Science Students*. Oxford: Blackwell.

Fuller, S. (1998) *Being There with Thomas Kuhn: A Philosophical History for Our Times*. Chicago, IL: University of Chicago Press.

Gellner, E. (1988) *Plough, Sword, Book*. Chicago, IL: University of Chicago Press.

Gerschenkron, A. (1962) *Economic Backwardness in Historical Perspective*. Cambridge, MA: Harvard University Press.

Gilbert N. and Mulkay, M. (1984) *Opening Pandora's Box*. Cambridge: Cambridge University Press.

Gjertsen, D. (1989) *Science and Philosophy: Past and Present*. Harmondsworth: Penguin.

Gong, G. (1984) *The Standard of 'Civilization' in International Society*. Oxford: Oxford University Press.

Goodman, D. and Russell, C. (1991) *The Rise of Scientific Europe, 1500–1800*. Milton Keynes: Open University Press.

Goodson, I. (1988) *The Making of Curriculum*. London: Falmer Press.

Gould, S. J. (1989) *Wonderful Life*. Harmondsworth: Penguin.

Graff, H. (1987). *The Legacies of Literacy*. Bloomington, IN: Indiana University Press.

Grant, E. (1977) *Physical Science in the Middle Ages*. Cambridge: Cambridge University Press

Gross, A. and Keith, W. (eds) (1996) *Rhetorical Hermeneutics: Invention and Interpretation in the Age of Science*. Albany, NY: SUNY Press.

Hacking, I. (ed.) (1982) *Scientific Revolutions*. Oxford: Oxford University Press.

Halsey, A. H. (1992) *The Decline of Donnish Dominion*, 2nd edn. Oxford: Clarendon Press.

Harding, S. (1991) *Whose Science? Whose Knowledge?* Ithaca, NY: Cornell University Press.

Harding, S. (ed.) (1993) *The Racial Economy of the Science*. Bloomington, IN: Indiana University Press.

Hedges, L. (1987) 'How hard is hard science, how soft is soft science?', *American Psychologist* **42**, 443–55.

Hempel, C. (1965) *Aspects of Scientific Explanation*. New York: Harper & Row.

Hess, D. (1993) *Science in the New Age*. Madison, WI: University of Wisconsin Press.

Hess, D. (1995) *Science & Technology in a Multicultural World*. New York: Columbia University Press.

Hollis, M. and Lukes, S. (eds) (1982) *Rationality and Relativism*. Cambridge, MA: MIT Press.

Holmes, B. and McLean, M. (1990) *The Curriculum: A Comparative Perspective*. London: Routledge.

Hooker, C. (1987) *A Realistic Theory of Science*. Albany, NY: SUNY Press.

Huff, T. (1993) *The Rise of Early Modern Science: Islam, China and the West*. Cambridge: Cambridge University Press.

Hull, D. (1988) *Science as a Process*. Chicago, IL: University of Chicago Press.

Humphrey, G. (1951) *Thinking*. London: Methuen.

Inkster, I. (1991) *Science and Technology in History: An Approach to Industrial Development*. London: Macmillan.

Johnson, J. (1990) *The Kaiser's Chemists: Science and Modernization in Imperial Germany*. Chapel Hill, NC: University of North Carolina Press.

Journet, D. (1995) 'Synthesizing disciplinary narratives: George Gaylord Simpson's *Tempo and Mode in Evolution*', *Social Epistemology*, **9**, 113–50.

Katz, R. L. (1986) 'Measurement and cross-national comparisons of the information work force', *The Information Society*, **4**, 231–78.

Keddie, N. (1968) *An Islamic Response to Imperialism: Political and Religious Writings of Sayyid ad-Din 'al-Afghani'*. Berkeley, CA: University of California Press.

Keller, E. F. (1985) *Reflections on Science and Gender*. New Haven, CT: Yale University Press.

Kitcher, P. (1993) *The Advancement of Science*. Oxford: Oxford University Press.

Kleinman, D. (1995) *Politics on the Endless Frontier: Postwar Research Policy in the United States*. Durham, NC: Duke University Press.

Kling, R. (ed.) (1995) 'Special issue: electronic journals and scholarly publishing', *The Information Society*, **11**, 237–344.

Knorr-Cetina, K. (1981) *The Manufacture of Knowledge*. Oxford: Pergamon Press.

Kuhn, T. (1970) *The Structure of Scientific Revolutions*, 2nd edn. Chicago, IL: University of Chicago Press.

Kuhn, T. (1977) *The Essential Tension*. Chicago, IL: University of Chicago Press.

Lakatos, I. and Musgrave, A. (eds) (1970) *Criticism and the Growth of Knowledge*. Cambridge: Cambridge University Press.

Latour, B. (1987) *Science in Action*. Cambridge, MA: Harvard University Press.

Latour, B. and Woolgar, S. (1986) *Laboratory Life: The Construction of Scientific Facts*, 2nd edn. Princeton, NJ: Princeton University Press.

Laudan, L. (1977) *Progress and Its Problems*. Berkeley, CA: University of California Press.

Leach, J. (1996) 'Healing and the Word: Sophistical Rhetoric and Hippocratic Medicine in Classical Antiquity', PhD dissertation, University of Pittsburgh.

LeGoff, J. (1993) *Intellectuals in the Middle Ages*. Oxford: Blackwell.

Leplin, J. (ed.) (1984) *Scientific Realism*. Berkeley, CA: University of California Press.

Lewenstein, B. (ed.) (1992) *When Science Meets the Public*, Washington, DC: American Association for the Advancement of Science.

Lewis, B. (1982) *The Muslim Discovery of Europe*. New York: Random House.

Lindley, D. (1993) *The End of Physics*. New York: Basic Books.

MacIntyre, A. (1970) 'Is understanding religion compatible with believing?' in B. Wilson (ed.), *Rationality*. Oxford: Blackwell.

MacKenzie, D. (1995) *Knowing Machines*. Cambridge, MA: MIT Press.

Malinowski, B. (1954) *Magic, Science and Religion*. Garden City, NY: Doubleday.

Mannheim, K. (1936) *Ideology and Utopia*. London: Routledge & Kegan Paul.

Matthews, J. R. (1995) *The Quest for Medical Certainty*. Princeton, NJ: Princeton University Press.

McCloskey, M. (1983) 'Intuitive physics', *Scientific American*, **4**, 122–30.

McGuire, J. E. and Rattansi, P. M. (1966) 'Newton and the pipes of Pan', *Notes and Records of the Royal Society*, **21**, 109–30.

Merton, R. (1970) *Science and Technology in Seventeenth Century England*. New York: Harper & Row.

Merton, R. (1973) *The Sociology of Science*. Chicago, IL: University of Chicago Press.

Midgley, M. (1992) *Science as Salvation*. London: Routledge.

Mirowski, P. (1989) *More Heat than Light*. Cambridge: Cambridge University Press.

Montgomery, S. (1995) *The Scientific Voice*. New York: Guilford Press.

Morris-Suzuki, T. (1994) *The Technological Transformation of Japan*. Cambridge: Cambridge University Press.

Mulkay, M. (1990) *Sociology of Science*. Bloomington, IN: Indiana University Press.

Needham, J. (1969) *The Grand Titration: Science and Society in East and West*. London: Allen & Unwin.

Parfit, D. (1984) *Reasons and Persons*. Oxford: Oxford University Press.

Peters, D. and Ceci, S. (1982) 'Peer-review practices of psychological journals: the fate of published articles submitted again', *Behavior and Brain Sciences*, **5**, 187–225.

Pinch, T. (1990) 'The sociology of the scientific community', in R. Olby, G. Cantor, J. Christie, and M. Hodge (eds), *Companion to the History of Modern Science*. London: Routledge.

Polanyi, M. (1957) *Personal Knowledge*. Chicago: University of Chicago Press.

Popper, K. (1959) *The Logic of Scientific Discovery*. New York: Harper & Row.

Popper, K. (1972) *Objective Knowledge*. Oxford: Oxford University Press.

Price, C. (1993) *Time, Discounting and Value*. Oxford: Blackwell.

Price, D. De Solla (1970) 'Citation measures of hard science, soft science, technology and nonscience', in C. Nelson and D. Pollock (eds), *Communication among Scientists and Engineers*. Lexington, MA: Heath & Co.

Price, D. De Solla (1978) 'Toward a model for science indicators', in Y. Elkana *et al.* (eds), *Toward a Metric of Science: The Advent of Science Indicators*. New York: Wiley-Interscience.

Price, D. De Solla (1986) *Little Science, Big Science . . . and Beyond*, 2nd edn. New York: Columbia University Press.

Proctor, R. (1991) *Value-Free Science? The Purity and Power of Knowledge*. Cambridge, MA: Harvard University Press.

Pyenson, L. (1993a) 'Prerogatives of European intellect: historians of science and the promotion of Western civilization', *History of Science*, **31**, 289–315.

Pyenson, L. (1993b) 'The ideology of Western rationality: history of science and the European civilizing mission', *Science and Education*, **2**, 329–43.

Rahman, F. (1982) *Islam and Modernity*. Chicago, IL: University of Chicago Press.

Rahmena, A. (ed.) (1994) *Pioneers of Islamic Revival*. London: Zed Books.

Raj, K. (1988) 'Images of knowledge, social organization, and attitudes in an Indian physics department', *Science in Context*, **2**, 317–89.

Ralston, D. (1990) *Importing the European army: The introduction of European military techniques and institutions into the extra-European world, 1600–1914*. Chicago, IL: University of Chicago Press.

Ravetz, J. (1971) *Scientific Knowledge and Its Social Problems*. Oxford: Oxford University Press.

Rawls, J. (1971) *A Theory of Justice*. Cambridge, MA: Harvard University Press.

Rescher, N. (1984) *The Limits of Science*. Berkeley, CA: University of California Press.

Ringer, F. (1979) *Education and Society in Modern Europe*. Bloomington, IN: Indiana University Press.

Said, E. (1978) *Orientalism*. New York: Random House.

Sardar, Z. (1989) *Explorations in Islamic Science*. London: Mansell.

Schmidt, J. (ed.) (1996) *What is Enlightenment? Eighteenth Century Answers and Twentieth Century Questions*. Berkeley: University of California Press.

Schumpeter, J. (1945) *Capitalism, Socialism and Democracy*. 2nd edn. New York: Harper & Row.

Shadish, W. and Fuller, S. (eds) (1993) *The Social Psychology of Science*. New York: Guilford Press.

Shahidullah, S. (1991) *Capacity-Building in Science and Technology in the Third World*. Boulder, CO: Westview Press.

Shapin, S. and Schaffer, S. (1985) *Leviathan and the Air-Pump*. Princeton, NJ: Princeton University Press.

Sivin, N. (1982) 'Why the scientific revolution did not take place in China – or didn't it?', *Chinese Science* 5, 45–66.

Small, H. (1975) 'A citation model for scientific specialties', *Proceedings of the American Society for Information Science*, 12, 34–5.

Sorell, T. (1991) *Scientism*. London: Routledge.

Stebbing, L. S. (1937) *Philosophy and the Physicists*. New York: Dover.

Sternberg, R. (1990) *Metaphors of Mind*. Cambridge: Cambridge University Press.

Taylor, C. A. (1996) *Defining Science*. Madison, WI: University of Wisconsin Press.

Turner, S. and Daryl, C. (1976) 'Another appraisal of Ortega, the Coles, and science policy: the Ecclesiastes hypothesis', *Social Science Information*, 15, 657–62.

Van Sertima, I. (ed.) (1986) *Blacks in Science: Ancient and Modern*. New Brunswick, NJ: Transaction Books.

Vincenti, W. (1990) *What Engineers Know and How They Know It: Analytical Studies from Aeronautical History*. Baltimore: Johns Hopkins University Press.

Wallerstein, I. (1991) *Unthinking Social Science: The Limits of Nineteenth Century Paradigms*. Oxford: Blackwell.

Weatherford, J. (1988) *Indian Givers*. New York: Crown Publishers.

Weber, M. (1958) 'Science as a vocation', in H. Gerth and C. W. Mills (eds), *From Max Weber*. Oxford: Oxford University Press.

Weber, M. (1965) *The Sociology of Religion*. Boston, MA: Beacon Press.

Weinberg, S. (1992) *Dreams of a Final Theory*. New York: Pantheon Books.

Winner, L. (1977) *Autonomous Technology*. Cambridge, MA: MIT Press.
Wittfogel, K. (1957) *Oriental Despotism: A Comparative Study of Total Power*. New Haven, CT: Yale University Press.
Wittgenstein, L. (1952) *Philosophical Investigations*. Oxford: Blackwell.
Wolpert, L. (1992) *The Unnatural Nature of Science*. London: Faber & Faber.
Wouters, P. (1994) 'The citation culture: how the citation came out of the bag and why it is hard to return it', Paper delivered at the annual meeting of the Society for Social Studies of Science, New Orleans.
Yeo, R. (1993) *Defining Science*. Cambridge: Cambridge University Press.
Zeldin, T. (1967) 'Higher education in France: 1848–1940', in W. Laqueur and G. Mosse (eds) *Education and Social Structure in the Twentieth Century*. New York: Harper & Row.

Index

adaptive preference formation, 46,
  99–100
African science, 90–3, 111
American science, 4, 59–60, 69,
  120, 124, 126, 131
anthropology, 10, 14, 31, 32, 40, 42,
  44–7, 52, 60, 64, 75, 141
Arabic science, *see* Islam
Aristotle, 28, 57, 82–3, 93–4, 103,
  115, 128
astronomy, 96, 119–20, 125, 143
autonomy of science, 6, 8, 10, 67,
  76, 82, 88, 90, 103–4, 106–7,
  121, 125, 131–2
Averroës, 20, 112, 114–21

backwardness in science, 88, 114
Big Science, 7, 50, 68, 72–4, 109,
  141–2
biology, 8, 13–14, 16–17, 19, 41, 46,
  58, 118, 121
Boyle, R., 20–2, 51, 86
British science, 1, 48, 64, 93, 95, 98,
  110, 112, 120, 125, 139

capitalism, 7, 26, 29, 37, 50, 67,
  102–4, 123, 139
Catholicism, 26, 42, 93, 97, 115, 120
chemistry, 2, 37–8, 41, 44, 55, 61,
  66, 69, 88–9, 125, 141
Chinese science, 66, 83–5, 87, 106,
  114, 120, 128–9, 132, 137–8,
  140, 143–4
Christianity, 43, 58, 60–2, 107, 109,
  111–15, 117–19, 127–8, 139
civilization, 44–5, 80, 85, 104, 119,
  137–40
colonialism, *see* imperialism
computers, 29, 69, 133
Copernicus, N., 118–20, 127
Creation science, 58, 116–17
criticism in science, 4–7, 10, 21–6,
  29, 32, 42, 47, 55, 59–60, 67–8,
  76, 84–6, 88, 92, 94, 100, 111,
  120, 126–7, 130–1, 142–3

Darwin, C., 13–15, 17, 22, 33, 51,
  54, 67–8, 82, 125, 127, 142
democracy and science, 4–7, 9, 21,
  23, 32, 34, 59–60, 70, 91, 98,
  120, 127, 138
Dewey, J., 4, 12, 34
discounting the future, *see* time-
  discounting in science
Double Truth Doctrine, *see*
  Averroës
Duhem, P., 83, 118

ecology, *see* environmental science
economics, 3, 5, 7, 13, 29, 31, 37, 46,
  48, 52–3, 60–1, 70, 72, 83, 95,
  101–4, 108, 122, 132, 134, 139,
  142–3